CHARTING A COURSE
OF DISCIPLESHIP

A Workbook on Christian Discipleship

TERESA GILBERT, PATTY JOHANSEN, & JAY REGENNITTER

REVISED BY DELIA HALVERSON

ISBN 978-0-88177-608-9

CONTENTS

Y.B.H.

"Yes, But How?"

This question is what we heard from many United Methodist churches—small, large, rural, urban, geographically and ethnically diverse. "Yes, we understand the mission of the church is to 'make disciples for the transformation of the world.' But how do we do this? What does 'making disciples' look like? What is a disciple anyway? What are some practical tools we can use to be more effective? We have many programs already—how do we know they are really helping people to grow in faith? Help!"

The leaders of the Illinois Great Rivers Annual Conference heard these questions and pledged to focus time and energy on equipping congregations to develop intentional systems for forming disciples. Partnering with the General Board of Discipleship, they devoted countless hours and several years in developing a process that guides a congregation in taking seriously the task of making disciples. This conference undertook a journey to explore what was already working—and not working—in disciple formation. The commitment involved listening, dreaming, praying, testing, succeeding, failing, learning, and trying again. The result is Charting a Course of Discipleship, a step-by-step approach that will help any congregation design a disciple formation process that is effective for their particular context.

> **This book helps churches answer:**
>
> • How do we fulfill what Jesus commanded?
>
> • How do we make and grow disciples?

This book is more of a workbook than a philosophical treatment of disciple formation. Based on solid and tested principles, its intent is to guide a congregation through a series of steps that will help them be clear about the mission of the church, assess their current reality in forming disciples, dream what might be possible, and then either build or improve the way they help persons come to and grow in the Christian faith. The approach is built upon John Wesley's understanding of grace and the need for different levels of support at different stages of faith development.

Numerous congregations of various sizes and locations around the country have used the process, resulting in excitement for forming disciples. The steps have led congregations to clarity about what they mean when they say "disciple" and how they can help people, whatever their stage of faith, grow in their love of God and neighbor. Using the process has brought new life and energy to congregations as they have designed creative ways to carry out the Great Commission in Matthew 28.

Caution: Be warned that this is a "messy" process. Working on disciple formation as a congregation is rarely smooth. People don't always agree on what it means to be a disciple, who should be one, and what ministries and approaches are most important. Any congregation that decides to use this workbook should expect some messiness! But the results are well worth the journey.

Yes, but how?

Yes. We understand that the mission of the church is to make disciples of Jesus Christ to transform the world. How? Use Charting a Course of Discipleship to lead your congregation to new levels of effectiveness in helping persons come to faith and grow as disciples of Jesus Christ.

—Donna Gaither, Team Leader for GBOD & Illinois Great Rivers Project

OVERVIEW

Go to the people of all nations and make them my disciples. Baptize them in the name of the Father, the Son, and the Holy Spirit, and teach them to do everything I have told you. I will be with you always, even until the end of the world.

(Matthew 28:19-20, CEV)

According to the Gospel of Matthew, Jesus gave this command to his disciples the last time he was with them. It is as important today as it was then. We believe that the development of a disciple formation process in a local church can quench thirsting spirits, fill souls with living water, and aid your congregation in effectively fulfilling its mission. As the Holy Spirit guides and directs your church, let this study help you chart your unique course for forming disciples in your context.

You have this workbook because you have discerned one of two things:

- Your church could benefit from the development of a disciple formation plan for your congregation's context

OR

- Your church is already involved in discipleship ministries but needs to develop a better approach to help people grow deeper in faith.

Do individuals in your church understand exactly what a disciple is?

Do individuals in your church understand discipleship as a lifelong journey?

Do individuals in your church know specific things they can do to grow deeper as disciples of Jesus Christ?

A disciple formation process can help congregations make and grow disciples of Jesus Christ, in fulfillment of Christ's commission to us. By working with this book, your church is taking seriously the call to make disciples.

Discipleship Formation

- Is not optional.
- Is messy.
- Is the work of the individual, the congregation, and God.
- Will look different in each context.
- Is for the transformation of the world.
- Above all, is intentional.

What Is the Book About?

Charting a Course for Discipleship provides a means for local churches to initiate or improve intentional disciple formation. It will help churches to:

• Develop leaders who practice the means of grace in their own lives and enable others to do the same

AND

• Design a disciple formation process within their own congregation that is contextually relevant to their situation.

This book will get you started, and then you will develop your own course of discipleship. This plan is not a prescription or a "cookie-cutter" approach. Use it the way that is most effective for your congregation. You may choose to work through it step by step, or you may choose specific discovery activities that will help your church become more vital and effective. Such decisions will come about as you work with this material.

The steps may **take 3, 6, or 12 months** for you to work through. In fact, some churches that have used it began with a very small group and took three months to prayerfully put together the larger team, being sure that those asked to be on it saw the opportunity as a calling for their ministry.

This process is like a **road map or nautical chart**. Study it all first, then determine your way. The journey is important! At the end you should have:

• An understanding of the characteristics of a disciple;

• An understanding of where your congregation excels or needs work in making disciples;

• A plan for individuals and the community to grow in their faith as disciples of Jesus Christ.

Who Will Need the Book?

The book is your guide. The leader/facilitator, pastor, and co-leader will need to have copies. Participants are not required to have the book, although having it may be helpful; but the facilitator can provide their materials as handouts copied from it.

What Are the Steps?

Step 1 – GATHERING THE CREW: Whom Is God Calling?

First, you will need to search out those whom God is calling to work together on this venture. This step will give you suggestions for selecting and forming the team. You will be ready to move to Step 2 when you have selected your team.

> **Each step may take more than one session.**

Step 2 – SETTING OUR SIGHTS: Getting Started

Without community you can do nothing. This step will help you build Christian community among the team members, reinforcing their calling as you set your sights on the course ahead. You will be ready to move on after your first team meeting.

Step 3 – PLANNING THE VOYAGE: Discovering the Mission

At this stage the focus is on helping the team grow in understanding of the mission of The United Methodist Church and how a disciple formation process will flow from it. Later, the team will bring the whole congregation into this understanding. You will be ready for Step 4 when the team understands the mission of the church and the role of forming disciples to accomplish the mission.

Step 4 – FINDING TRUE NORTH: What's a Disciple?

The goal here is to discover and express an understanding of the meaning of the word disciple, including a list of spiritual practices of a disciple, which will be unique to the context of your local church. You will be ready to move to the next step when the team comfortably describes a disciple and has engaged the congregation in the discussion.

Step 5 – STUDYING THE MAPS: Looking Around

Important at this stage is looking at several examples, both historical and current, of disciple forming processes and identifying the necessary components of a healthy approach. You will move to Step 6 when the team understands growing in faith as a life-long journey.

Step 6 – CHECKING OUR BEARINGS: What Are We Doing?

In this step you will assess the current level of disciple making in your congregation. The book will introduce some tools you can use to identify components of your present efforts. **(This step, especially, may take a longer session, or two sessions. Plan ahead for this.)** You will move on when the team has a grasp of what your congregation currently does, as it relates to growing as disciples.

Step 7 – TURNING THE COURSE: Where Do We Want to Go?

Here you will specifically listen to God's calling to your church, considering the way your current reality, your insights from Scripture, your context, and the values of your congregation will move toward transformation of people's lives. You may decide to include a larger group in some of this step. As the team develops a clear vision for the future, you will move to the next step.

Step 8 – ADJUSTING THE BEARINGS: How Will We Get There?

At this point, you are trying to move from where you are now toward God's vision for your church. As the team develops a plan to improve your disciple making, excitement will build and specific details will emerge. The plan you develop will be a structure allowing for individual growth, creative plans, and new ideas. When the group has developed your framework for helping all people grow, you will move to the next step.

Step 9 – SHARING THE VOYAGE: Who's Going With Us?

Inviting people to own and engage in the congregation's disciple formation process naturally flows from the team's excitement about the plan. You have already communicated with and involved others in the congregation at every phase of charting the course; now the team will help people find their place in the disciple formation plan. At this step, you may consider a "launch" of the vision or you may decide to make changes incrementally. After you have communicated and begun new opportunities for growth, you will move to the next step.

Step 10 – CONTINUING THE VOYAGE: Keeping It Going

This step looks to the future with the goal of establishing a culture of disciple formation in your church. The team will plan ways to continue and also to intentionally renew your discipleship system. The team will decide how to evaluate and monitor the work started and do succession planning, as they take time to ensure the long-term future of making disciples for Jesus Christ through your congregation.

What Else Is in This Guide?

- INDIVIDUAL PREPARATION: The handouts for individual preparation are at the end of each step so the facilitator can make copies to give the participants. Each handout will have a centering prayer and Scripture to use in the opening worship. **You will need to mail out the first handout** so that the team members can read it before coming to the initial meeting. Other handouts can be distributed when you complete a step so that people can prepare for the next one. Stress the importance of the team members reading and reflecting on the handouts before coming to the meeting.

- OPENING WORSHIP: Each section of this guide will begin with an opening worship, including a centering prayer. The centering prayer and other items that the team will say together will be printed in the handouts for individual preparation. Team members will use the prayer as they prepare and as the group comes together.

- STEP AT A GLANCE: The Step at a Glance section lists the goals, the suggested plan for the meeting, and any preparation necessary for that particular step's activities.

- BIBLE STUDY: You will find Bible studies to copy at the end of each step. The meeting plans will give suggestions for facilitating the studies during the meetings. Some may be shared with other groups in the church or printed in a newsletter or online for the whole congregation.

- DISCOVERY ACTIVITY: Each step includes suggested discovery activities for your meetings. They move your planning group along the journey.

What Do the Icons Indicate?

 ROLE OF THE TEAM LEADER/FACILITATOR: These suggestions will be for those leading the team. They will include tips for working with the team members, seeing that specific things are done, or following through on something.

 ROLE OF THE TEAM: When we say "the team," we are referring to the initial group of twelve or so who committed to the task. At times throughout your work together, the team may need to take a specific role in guiding the congregation.

 ROLE OF THE PASTOR: You will definitely want cooperation from the clergy and lay leadership of your church. The pastor is in a strategic position to remind the whole congregation of the church's mission.

 INVITING THE CONGREGATION: This section will give suggestions on how you can involve the whole congregation in the excitement of charting the course.

 CHECK YOUR BEARINGS: This icon is a reminder to evaluate what you have done thus far and to assess how the team members are doing.

 YOUR CHURCH: This icon will indicate something of particular importance especially to small churches or to very large ones.

Step 1

GATHERING THE CREW

Whom Is God Calling?

> The aim of this step is to search out those whom God is calling to work together on this venture. This step will give you suggestions for selecting and forming the team.

The **leader** or **facilitator** must be one who is committed to the church, already an active disciple, passionate about the mission of the congregation, a "people person," a conciliator and reconciler, and an enthusiastic and tenacious individual! Does this mean the pastor? Not necessarily. In fact, a strong lay leader might encourage more persons to become involved and "catch the idea" better than the pastor (who, unfortunately, might be seen as "pushing the latest program that's come down the pipeline").

Of course, the **pastor** must be involved every step of the way, but assuming that the pastor is the only one who can facilitate the study and use of this workbook is to deny the great talent, commitment, and enthusiasm resident among the lay members of your congregation—even if that congregation consists of only ten individuals!

Whether you are a layperson, pastor, committee chair, or staff member, the purpose of this book is to involve you and your congregation in

1. Understanding just what making disciples is and involves,

2. Evaluating your present efforts at making disciples, and

3. Planning specific disciple-making ministries for the future.

Key leaders, a small handpicked group, and eventually the whole congregation will discuss the ideas! As people claim their faith and live as disciples, the excitement will spread from the small group to a larger group, and your whole congregation will soon become involved in becoming and making disciples.

Most churches who have worked on such a program have found it most effective to work with an ad hoc group of committed persons drawn together just for this purpose. However, at some point you may involve:

- The church council or council on ministries, or whatever group that is responsible for the ministries of your congregation.

- An adult Sunday school class, or several adult classes, and perhaps a youth class or two thrown in as well.

- A weeknight study group of folks drawn from your congregation.

- A women or men's group in your congregation.

> Remember, the small leader-ship group must become excited before the ideas can spread to the congregation!

 INVITING THE CONGREGATION: Communicating to the congregation from time to time is critical as you move forward. This work you are doing is not some big secret to suddenly be revealed! The congregation needs ownership. At what point you involve them will depend on your decisions as a team. This guidebook provides several suggestions, but you will know when it is best for you to involve certain groups or the whole congregation.

 YOUR CHURCH: If yours is a **small congregation**, you may begin with a group of two or three and then involve the whole congregation. In a really **large-membership congregation**, consider having a few selected staff and laypersons of the church work through the book before including others in the study.

We hope you're getting the point here. The more persons you can eventually involve in this study and discussion, the better! But begin small in order to form a committed group, who can then spread the excitement about what you develop.

On Developing a Team

- The team you are building for your church has one purpose: the development of ways of forming disciples in a manner that is unique to your church's context.

- Your team should have a maximum of twelve persons, including the pastor. This size will allow for efficiency in decision-making, accountability, and care for one another.

- Your team may divide into sub-teams, which may in turn build new teams for accomplishing a specific task, function, or sub-purpose. You need an intentional system for individual sub-teams to be connected and communicate; generally that will happen through the team leadership.

- Your team will be engaging in discernment about the development of the disciple formation process, at points inviting the congregation to seek discernment with the team.

- Your team will be developing a plan for communication with the congregation throughout the implementation of this plan, as a means of continuing to build buy-in.

- Your team will need to set regular times to meet. Expect it to take a few times for members to establish the calendar. Leadership may need to help people say "no" to other church activities in order to give attention to this task.

- Your team may need to examine your church's current practices regarding how and why decisions are made. What drives decisions? Is it money, past practice, or something else? What changes could be or might be needed and implemented?

Calling Your Small Team

- Find one or two others who recognize the need for charting a course of discipleship in your church, and rely on the Holy Spirit to guide you as you discuss who should be on the initial team. Discerning whom to invite may take some time.

- Twelve is usually considered an ideal number in order to have a variety of people yet be small enough for everyone to be heard. Jesus set an example with twelve disciples.

- Don't start your selection with names but with the gifts needed for such a team. Then identify people who have those gifts and graces.

- Surround all of your decisions in prayer. Pray over each of the gifts identified and then over each name suggested. Be sure that God is leading you to call each person. Your prayer does not guarantee that persons will accept your call. They know their own situations and must feel God calling them to accept this position at this particular time in their lives.

- Explain to those you call that you see gifts in them that will contribute to this team. Tell them that their own faith will grow as a result of your work together. Explain that the commitment is important and that it may take several months or even up to a year. Then ask them to pray about the invitation. Let them know that you will talk with them on a specific date to ask whether they see God calling them to join this team.

- Consider co-leaders for the team. The up-front leadership may or may not include a staff member, but a staff member should be a part of the planning for each session.

Suggestions for the Team Meetings

- The first meetings will not only be for information but also for team building. You may decide to have a meal together at the first meeting or at some other points during your study. Let any meals be simple. Eating together does help to form relationships. Jesus recognized this.

- Set a time for study sessions. Start on time and end at the promised time. Recognize that some steps may take longer than others—Step 5, for example. Read the whole manual to determine your time-frames.

- Ask each team member to select a prayer partner in the congregation who will pray for the team and for that team member specifically.

• Begin each session with an opening worship similar to that suggested in the book.

• Create a "worshipful work" attitude about the meetings. Encourage the team members to see their work as an offering to God. Some leaders have used a form of worship for their meetings, beginning with praise, followed by confession, and even labeling the decision-making time as their "offering."

• Pray not only at the beginning and ending of every session, but stop for prayer when important decisions are about to be made. You might even ask team members to go quietly into the sanctuary (or some other quiet place) and pray alone for a period of time before such a decision. And if the group seems to reach an impasse, pray! Let group members offer prayers. Call for silent prayer. Surround your sessions with prayer.

• Set up your meeting room so that all can see one another. Tables in a horseshoe or square shape are appropriate, or if you don't use tables, place the chairs in a semicircle or circle.

• Have a chalkboard, whiteboard, or newsprint available. Use it!

• Ask at least one person to take notes on your discussions. It may be better if two or three take notes. That way, each note-taker can contribute to the discussion as well as capturing the notes. Don't try to combine the notes into one set of minutes. Hear from each note-taker at the end of a session and at the beginning of the next session. The richness of your discussion will be revealed!

• Realize that change will create conflict. When this happens go to God in prayer individually and as a group.

• Make decisions; then move on! Try to make decisions by consensus; that is, an idea or decision is discussed and tweaked until everyone "buys into it." Voting creates winners and losers. By working toward consensus, everyone wins!

• When you get stuck, first make sure that everyone understands just what the other is saying. Ask persons to repeat their statement in other words, helping the speaker and listener both to hear what is being said.

• Two words of advice worth remembering:

1. Once you give an idea to the group, the idea belongs to the group, not to you anymore. The group can change, adapt, accept, or reject the idea because the idea now belongs to the group.

2. A group can get done anything they need to as long as no one cares who gets credit for it!

Resources

During your work together, you will want to use discernment and consensus in making decisions instead of "taking a vote." Yes and no votes only divide a group. For help with group discernment, consult these resources, which may be in your church's or pastor's library:

Practicing Our Faith, edited by Dorothy C. Bass, Jossey-Bass (1997); Chapter 8, "Discernment" by Frank Rogers Jr.

Discerning God's Will Together, by Danny E. Morris and Charles M. Olsen, Upper Room Books (1997); Chapter 4.

Transforming Church Boards, by Charles M. Olsen, An Alban Institute Publication (1995); Chapter 5.

LEADER/FACILITATOR: Invite and confirm team members, set the time and place for your first meeting, and distribute copies of the Individual Preparation (next page) to the people on the team so they can prepare for the first meeting.

(Handout)

Individual Preparation

Read this ahead of time, and bring it with you to our first meeting.

Centering Prayer

Great and amazing God, as we begin our discernment, lead us in making our work worshipful throughout our time together. As we focus and gain perspective on who you call us to be and as we seek to reclaim the mission of making disciples, embrace us. Keep us grounded in your Word during our work together. Be the focus of all we say and do. We pray in the name of the one who gave us the Great Commission, Jesus the Christ. Amen.

Scripture

As a deer gets thirsty for streams of water,
I truly am thirsty for you, my God.
In my heart, I am thirsty for you, the living God.
When will I see your face?

(Psalm 42:1-2, CEV)

Reflection

Respond in writing to these questions:

• When have you felt a true thirst/yearning for God's presence?

• How have you expressed that yearning?

• What has helped you grow closer to God?

• Can you think of persons in our church who long for God but do not know how to grow as a disciple?

• The word, Immanuel, means "God with us." When have you felt that God was with you in a specific situation?

• When have you felt that God was with our church in a specific situation?

The goal of our first session is to get to know one another better and create a common focus together.

May the Lord make your love increase and overflow for each other
and for everyone else, just as ours does for you.

(1 Thessalonians 3:12, NIV)

Step 2

SETTING OUR SIGHTS

Getting Started

> You now have your team in place. The aim of this step is to build a Christian community among the team members. Without this community you can do nothing. The team will recognize that God is already at work in their life and in your congregation. This step will also reinforce the calling of the team members as you set your sights on making disciples.

Great and amazing God,
As we begin our discernment, lead us in making our work worshipful throughout
our time together. As we focus and gain perspective on who you call us to be
and as we seek to reclaim the mission of making disciples, embrace us.
Keep us grounded in your Word always.
Be the focus of all we say and do.
We pray in the name of the one who gave us the Great Commission,
Jesus the Christ. Amen.

Step 2 at a Glance

Goals

- To build a strong team for developing an intentional plan for discipleship in your congregation.

- To better acquaint team members. Although your team members may know each other, this session will give them some insights into one another's spirituality.

- To recognize that although the group is made up of people with diverse gifts and talents, God can use those to bring together a great team with a great mission.

Possible Format

- Worship

- Discovery Activity 1

- Prayer Partners

- Timeline and Historical Profile

- Discovery Activity 2

- Bible Study

- Recognition of Gifts and Giver

- Covenant

- Closing

Preparation

- Place a candle and matches on the table. (Or use a battery-operated candle.)

- Make copies of the Bible study at the end of this session and of Individual Preparation for the next session.

- Arrange for a long paper, masking tape and markers or whiteboard and dry markers for timeline.

- Have 3 x 5 cards and pens or pencils available.

- If you choose the suggested option for celebrating gifts and talents, you will need colorful plaid cloth (some cut into small pieces) and hymnals or copies of the hymn: *Many Gifts, One Spirit* (#114 in *The United Methodist Hymnal*).

Worship

- Light the candle, telling the group that the candle reminds us that Christ is with us throughout our time together. Suggest that anyone may blow the candle out if at some time during the work together you do not act or speak as you would if Christ were physically present with you. After a few moments of prayer, relight the candle and resume your task in a more Christ-like way.

- Read the centering prayer from the Individual Preparation sheet together, or have someone read it while the group meditates.

- Ask where they have seen God at work in their lives or in the life of the church recently.

- Read together Psalm 42:1-2, as printed on the Individual Preparation sheet.

- Ask those who would like, to read some of the things they wrote on their Individual Preparation page:

    ❍ When have you felt a true yearning for God's presence?

    ❍ How have you expressed that yearning?

    ❍ What helped you grow closer to God?

    ❍ Can you think of persons in our church who may have such a yearning but do not know how to grow as a disciple?

- Emphasize the suggestion in the Individual Preparation that speaks of Immanuel being defined as God with us. Direct the discussion to recognition of times when you have felt that God was with your congregation in guiding you in specific things. Help the group realize that God is already with you in the congregation.

- Pray a prayer similar to this: Our God, we recognize the yearnings of each of us and of others in our church family. Help us understand your mission as a means of bringing us closer to you. Amen.

Discovery Activity 1

Ask persons to introduce themselves and, referring to their individual preparation, briefly tell of a time when they felt especially close to God.

Explain that God has been present, guiding the life of the church through history. Ask if any remember specific changes that came about in Christianity (or the church) over history and how God was evident during those times? They might mention some of the following:

- Jesus instigated many changes, such as having meals with "sinners."

- The early church allowed Gentiles to become members without circumcision.

- Faithful people were no longer required to meet solely in the Temple.

- Christians developed a scriptural attitude toward poor (St. Francis in Italy and St. Patrick in Ireland).

- We do not earn salvation by good deeds (Martin Luther).

- We can read and interpret the Bible ourselves.

- Worship services can be held in the streets and countryside (John Wesley).

- Christ's teachings can happen beyond the walls of the church building.

- Worship has many different forms.

As you end discussion, stress the importance of realizing that God is Immanuel, God with us in all we do.

Prayer Partners

Prayer partners can be important for any leader, and during this experience each person will choose someone outside this team to be his or her prayer partner. Prayer partners not only pray for the work ahead but also for their individual partners. The prayer partner need not be someone with a leadership role in the church. Often those who make the best prayer partners are persons who prefer not to be up front in leadership. Suggest that the team members ask prayer partners to:

- Pray at least once a day for their partner.

- Pray at some time during the meeting time. In order for this to happen the team member will need to be sure that the prayer partner knows the times of the meetings.

- Pray for all members of the team.

- Pray especially upon request of the team member for a special need.

Timeline and Historical Profile

Using some of the following questions, develop a timeline and historical profile for your congregation:

- Who were the founders and early spiritual leaders of our congregation?

- When have we had severe disagreements and what were they about?

- When might have we strayed from following God's direction?

- Who helped us see that God wanted us to go in a specific direction?

- When have we worked specifically with God in ministry and what did we do on those occasions?

- When have we failed to put emphasis on a specific age level or group of people?

- When did we recognize this lack and instigate a change?

- What are we doing now that is specifically a calling from God?

Discovery Activity 2

Hand out 3 x 5 cards and ask all the team members to write on the card at least one gift or talent that they feel God has given them. You can suggest gifts such as communication, math, organization, creativity, working with children or youth, teaching adults, praying for others, showing concern for others, knitting or crocheting prayer shawls or other use of their hands, cooking, computers, and so forth.

Ask each person to tell the group about one of his or her gifts.

Bible Study

Distribute the Bible study handout and work through it together. Have someone read the Scripture aloud. Encourage people to mark words or phrases that stand out for them.

Recognition of Gifts and Giver

Celebrate the gifts each member brings to the group in some manner. Here is one suggestion:

- Gather around a table that is draped with a colorful plaid cloth. (You will have used some of the same cloth to cut pieces for each person.)

- Sing or read the words of the hymn: *Many Gifts, One Spirit* (#114 in *The United Methodist Hymnal.*)

- Ask team members to place their 3 x 5 card with the listing of their talents on the table as an offering to God.

- Give each person a piece of a plaid fabric. Ask everyone to look at the colors and lines in the plaid and identify one color or line as his or her gift. Then pray this prayer or one similar:

God, we are many with varied gifts, which you have given us. We come to this mission of growing disciples for you with an understanding that we must work together, using the gifts that you have given us. We celebrate those gifts and depend on you to guide us through these weeks of study and work together. Amen.

Covenant

Create a covenant together to describe how you will work in a positive, supportive, and effective way.

Make a list of the ways you want to work together. As you group the ideas suggested by the team, write general statements to summarize an agreement to which everyone will commit. Before the next session, write this covenant so everyone can have a copy. You can also put it on a poster to display each time you meet.

During your meetings, refer to the covenant to remind yourselves of the bond you are developing. Here are some suggestions you might consider:

- On this team everyone has a right to be heard.

- Everyone has the right to ask questions.

- We will consider our team as a representation of the total congregation and will look to the needs of the whole congregation instead of those of individual team members.

- We will respect each member of the team.

- We will recognize that each member of the team is a child of God.

- Sometimes we may not agree, but we will strive to come to consensus.

- Even when we do not like another person's actions, we will try to show God's love for the person.

- We will pray before making major decisions.

- We will agree that being a member of this team is an important commitment, one that at times will require commitments to other things to be put aside.

Closing

Summarize the goal of getting to know one another and intentionally building a plan for discipleship, telling them that when you next meet you will discuss just what a disciple is.

Close in prayer, in whatever way seems appropriate, and read this benediction together: It is printed at the bottom of individual preparation handout.

May the Lord make your love increase and overflow for each other and for everyone else, just as ours does for you.

(1 Thessalonians 3:12, NIV)

Ask the team members to be in prayer about the mission and to ask their prayer partner to be in prayer. Hand out Individual Preparation for Step 3 and remind them to study it before the next session.

 LEADER/FACILITATOR: Encourage the team during this session and during the week. Between sessions, contact the team members and tell them that you are praying for them.

 TEAM: Pray for your upcoming times together and for your congregation.

 PASTOR: Consider having a dedication service during worship for the members of this team. Also, using the song "Go, Make of All Disciples" (#571 in The United Methodist Hymnal) in worship frequently during their work will draw attention to the mission.

 INVITING THE CONGREGATION: Communicate in some way to the congregation that you are beginning a study of how your church can grow in discipleship. Encourage all the members to think of the gifts that God has given them that might be used in ministry.

 CHECK YOUR BEARINGS: Did the team members find common grounds? Did they recognize that change has been a part of the church from the beginning? Does each team member have a prayer partner?

Bible Study for Step 2

Mark words or phrases that stand out for you as you listen to the reading:

The body of Christ has many different parts, just as any other body does. *Some of us are Jews, and others are Gentiles. Some of us are slaves, and others are free. But God's Spirit baptized each of us and made us part of the body of Christ. Now we each drink from that same Spirit.

Our bodies don't have just one part. They have many parts. Suppose a foot says, "I'm not a hand, and so I'm not part of the body" Wouldn't the foot still belong to the body? Or suppose an ear says, "I'm not an eye, and so I'm not part of the body." Wouldn't the ear still belong to the body? If our bodies were only an eye, we couldn't hear a thing. And if they were only an ear, we couldn't smell a thing. But God has put all parts of our body together in the way that he decided is best.

A body isn't really a body, unless there is more than one part. It takes many parts to make a single body…. Together you are the body of Christ. Each one of you is part of his body.

(1 Corinthians 12:12-20, 27, CEV)

*Verse 13 may also be translated, "God's Spirit is inside each of us, and all around us as well. So it doesn't matter that some of us are Jews and others are Gentiles and that some are slaves and others are free. Together we are one body."

• What words stand out to you? Is there anything in this new translation that gives you a fresh insight?

• How does this Scripture relate to our team?

• What qualities or characteristics are important for the team (or body) to function well?

• What qualities shall we hold ourselves accountable for?

Individual Preparation

Read this ahead of time, and bring it with you to our Step 3 meeting.

Centering Prayer

Our great God, you bring us together again to search for an understanding of what it means to be a disciple and follow Christ's teachings. We yearn for a church that is truly in step with Christ; a church that looks to your leading in everything that we do. We come with humble hearts, knowing that we cannot do this alone, and asking for your understanding, your guidance, and your grace. We pray in the name of the one who gave us the Great Commission, Jesus the Christ. Amen.

Scripture

> *Show me your paths and teach me to follow;*
> *guide me by your truth and instruct me.*
> *You keep me safe, and I always trust you.*

(Psalm 25:4-5, CEV)

Reflection

> The mission of the church is to make disciples of Jesus Christ for the transformation of the world. Local churches provide the most significant arena through which disciple-making occurs.
> (*The Book of Discipline of The United Methodist Church, 2012;* ¶120)

Wait!

Go back and read what's in that box again. You might have read it dozens of times before. But read it again. Read it slowly. Read it aloud. Read it again.

Now let's take a careful look at that statement, because each word is crucial.

The first word is *The*. Yes, we all know what that word means. But in this sentence that word carries a special meaning that we might miss. The sentence does not read "*A* mission" or "*One of the* missions." No, the statement reads loudly and clearly that the *one, single, exclusive* mission of the church is to make disciples of Jesus Christ for the transformation of the world.

What about the second word: *mission*? What is a mission? Put most simply and directly, **a mission is what we are supposed to be doing. It is the reason the church exists.** Our mission is our reason for being. It is the way we are to be spending ourselves. Our mission is the reason why we are here. Our mission is what we are about.

Our mission is not something we choose or define or modify. Our mission is given to us, and we are charged with and held responsible for fulfilling that mission. Our mission is not optional. Either we undertake our mission joyfully and enthusiastically, or we fail completely and endure the consequences of our failure.

Back up a minute: Did you catch the sentence above that says our mission is given to us by a higher authority? That higher authority is not *The Book of Discipline of The United Methodist Church* or the General Conference of The United Methodist Church or a group of bishops. That higher authority is God through Christ.

The United Methodist Church may put that mission into a set of words, but God gives us the mission. The church did not select or choose this mission. God charged the church with this mission. There are many persons and groups who help us carry out that mission, but God gave the mission to us, through Christ.

God
Through Christ

Church Council	The United Methodist Church
Pastors and Staff	Small Groups and Classes
Church Committees	Ministries With Children and Youth
Mission Opportunities	Prayer Groups and Bible Study

Make disciples of Jesus Christ for the transformation of the world

All of these people and structures help us carry out the mission. Many passages of Scripture could be cited to demonstrate this. The website for Vital Congregations (www.umvitalcongregations.org) says:

Vital congregations are:

Spirit-filled forward-learning communities of believers that welcome all people. (Galatians 3:28)

Places where disciples of Jesus Christ are made through the power of the Holy Spirit. (Matthew 28:18-20)

Communities that serve like Christ through justice and mercy ministries. (Micah 6:8; Luke 4:17-21)

A disciple of Jesus Christ:

• worships regularly

• helps make new disciples

• is engaged in growing in their faith

• is engaged in mission

• shares by giving in mission.

Whose mission is it? The church's. Remember, the church is not a building—but the people.

That suggests that the church on every level and in every form is charged with this mission.

That means that the church, no matter how we define it, has this mission.

That means that those worshiping in a huge cathedral, the congregation in a tiny rural frame building, the established congregation in the suburb, the little group of folks meeting in a storefront in the inner city, the new congregation that is just beginning to grow, the handful of related folks who have always called that crossroads building their church—all of these and every other example you can imagine—share in one common mission, one common calling, one common task given them by God through Christ.

- The twelve disciples received this challenge to make disciples.

- Paul and Timothy received this challenge.

- Early leaders of the church, such as Saint Augustine and Saint Francis, received this challenge.

- Martin Luther and John Wesley received this challenge.

- And now the challenge is OURS!

Our team is a part of that great cloud of witnesses who endeavor to carry out Christ's words:

Go to the people of all nations and make them my disciples. Baptize them in the name of the Father, the Son, and the Holy Spirit, and teach them to do everything I have told you. I will be with you always, even until the end of the world.

(Matthew 28:19-20, CEV)

How exciting is this?

Pray: Thank you, God for this opportunity to carry out this mission. Guide us as we listen to your calling. Amen.

Jeffrey D. Jones, in his book, *Traveling Together: A Guide for Disciple-forming Congregations*, Alban Institute, 2006, page 37 states that "A congregation is called to be…a community that makes/shapes/grows/nurtures/teaches/forms disciples."

Belonging to a church is more than sitting in worship, more than attending a Bible study, even more than membership.

The church, as a body of believers in Christ, does not choose its mission, does not decide whether or not it will accept this mission. Instead, one definition of the church is that *the church is a group of persons committed to fulfilling the mission given to those persons by God.*

And what is that mission?

Our mission is to make disciples of Jesus Christ for the transformation of the world.

Now we can quibble all we want over that verb *make*. That word does not mean that we "make" disciples as we would make a pie or a birdhouse. That word *make* means in this case that:

Our mission, our task, *the* reason we are here, is

to create those situations, those environments, and those conditions

in and through which

other persons can come to know Christ

and live according to the way of Christ.

God through Christ gives us our mission, which is to do all we can to make, form, and shape others into disciples of Jesus Christ.

And what is a disciple? That is a very big and a very important question! And we are going to devote a major section of our time together determining a functional description of the word *disciple*.

A *functional* definition is a description of what something *does*, not just what something *is*. Watch for it. Disciples are persons who do and act in certain ways; they are not persons who just say "yes" to something, then go their own way.

In this case we are talking about disciples of Jesus Christ, so these disciples will in some way do and act like Jesus. We'll explore this idea more in the next step.

Now let's look at the end of the first statement in the box above: **"…for the transformation of the world."** This carries out the mission that we see in the life of Christ. Think for a moment about a spiral. When you look at a spiral from one point, it appears to move from the outside in. But another view of the spiral can begin from the inner circle and move outward. That is the understanding of the rest of this sentence. We are to make disciples, not to make individual persons better for themselves, but so that they can move out into the world to transform the world. This action is no longer for self-interest or self-improvement, but one with a greater purpose. This mission statement for The United Methodist Church also follows the instructions Jesus gave his disciples when they asked him how to pray. His prayer included: *"Thy kingdom come, thy will be done, <u>on earth</u> as it is in heaven."* Jesus' life demonstrated this movement out into the world, transforming the world.

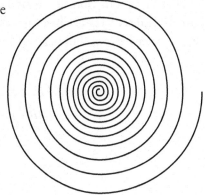

And so, we are about making disciples (preparing them) to move out into the world, to transform the world and to bring about God's kingdom on earth.

The rest of the statement in the box is **"Local churches provide the most significant arena through which disciple-making occurs."** That entire second sentence is a fancy way of saying that each congregation (not a church building but congregation; that is, a group of people!)—whether its membership is five or ten or one hundred or one thousand or ten thousand—is the prime place, the major place, the most important place in and through which persons come to be disciples. The mission is not carried out by a building; the mission is carried out by persons! We call a group of persons carrying out that mission of Christ a congregation!

Again, you and your church cannot opt out of the mission of making disciples. Making disciples is what churches do. A "church" that is not about disciple making is not a church. It may be a social club or a family group, perhaps, but it is not a church—for what churches do is make disciples.

➧ To be a church is to be about the mission of making disciples. That's a *functional* definition of a church.

Now, what about our church? Is it about making disciples? Is the congregation that gathers weekly in the building we call our church actively engaged in making disciples? Are the folks who make up our congregation disciples themselves?

That's what this study is all about. It matters not at all if our congregation consists of four to six people gathered to worship every other Sunday morning or if our congregation consists of three thousand people gathering in five services of worship every Sunday. The questions are the same:

- What is a disciple?
- Are we in this church here and now disciples?
- Are we as a congregation about the mission of making disciples?
- How can we be even more intentional about our mission of making disciples?
- How can we involve everyone in our entire congregation in the mission of making disciples?
- How can we steadily and constantly grow in our mission of making disciples?
- And a practical issue: How can we measure our growth and progress in our disciple-making mission?

That's what our work as a team is all about. It's about the mission of our congregation. And that mission is **to make disciples of Jesus Christ for the transformation of the world.** We will further discuss just what a disciple is in our later sessions, but begin thinking about it now.

May the Lord make your love increase and overflow for each other
and for everyone else, just as ours does for you.

(1 Thessalonians 3:12, NIV)

Step 3

PLANNING THE VOYAGE

Discovering the Mission

Christian community is forming among the team members whom God has called. Where do you go next? The aim of this step is to help the team embrace disciple making as a mission. The group will increase their understanding of the mission of The United Methodist Church and learn how a disciple-formation process flows from that mission. Later, they will bring the congregation into this understanding.

Our great God,

You bring us together again to search for an understanding of what it means

to be a disciple and follow Christ's teachings. We yearn for a church that is truly in

step with Christ; a church that looks to your leading in everything that we do.

We come with humble hearts, knowing that we cannot do this alone, and asking for

your understanding, your guidance, and your grace.

We pray in the name of the One who gave us the Great Commission,

Jesus the Christ. Amen.

Step 3 at a Glance

Goals

- To understand that making disciples is the biblical mission of every church.

- To find ways to help your congregation embrace this mission.

- To dedicate your team to the mission of leading your congregation through creating an intentional disciple formation process that will be transformational in your church and community.

Possible Format

- Worship

- Discovery Activity 1

- Bible Study

- Group Reflection on Individual Preparation

- Discovery Activity 2

- Closing

Preparation

- Place a candle and matches on the table. (Or use a battery-operated candle.)

- Make copies of the Bible study for this session and Individual Preparation for the next session.

- Provide newsprint, markers, and Bibles for each person or for persons to share.

- If you have a copy of *The Book of Discipline of The United Methodist Church*, use it to read the statement.

Worship

- Light the candle and remind the group of its meaning and that anyone may blow it out and relight it if at some time during your time together you do not act or speak as you would if Christ were physically here with you.

- Read the centering prayer on the Individual Preparation sheet together, or have someone read it while the group meditates.

- Ask where they have seen God at work in their lives or in the life of the church since last you met.

- Read together Psalm 25:4-5 from the Individual Preparation handout.

- Pray a prayer similar to this: Our God, we ask that you show us the paths that we must take to guide our church in making disciples. You alone know the best way we can go about this, and we look to you for that guidance. Amen.

Discovery Activity 1

This activity leads into the Bible study and is an important part of it.

- Ask team members to recall and share a time that they provided a service either intentionally or unintentionally; write these on a newsprint or whiteboard. Here are examples to launch the conversation, if needed:

  ❍ Teach a class

  ❍ Help with a school field trip or a church youth event

  ❍ Visit someone sick or sit with someone in a surgery waiting room

  ❍ Participate in a fundraiser for a charity

  ❍ Listen to someone who is hurting; share how you dealt with hard times or solved a problem

- Tell the group that they were in the act of making disciples in all of those situations. They were following Jesus' command in Matthew 28:16-20.

Bible Study

Distribute the Bible study handout and work through it together.

Group Reflection on Individual Preparation

Discuss thoughts about the handout, Individual Preparation for Step 3

Allow each participant to respond to the statements below; allow 5–10 minutes for each statement. (Capture thoughts on newsprint for future reference.)

- The statement from the *Discipline* does not read "A mission . . . " or "One of the missions . . . ." The statement reads loudly and clearly that the one, single, exclusive mission of the church is to make disciples of Jesus Christ.

- Put most simply and directly, a mission is what we are to be doing. Our mission is our reason for being. It is the cause for which we exist.

- Our mission is what we are given to do by a higher authority. Our mission is not something we choose or define or modify. Our mission is not optional. The higher authority is not *The Book of Discipline of The United Methodist Church*, or the General Conference of The United Methodist Church, or a group of bishops. That higher authority is God through Christ. It is God through Christ who gives us our mission.

Ask for any other discussion or revelations that they had when reading the preparation materials.

Discovery Activity 2

Read or have read Matthew 28:16-20.

Discuss these questions and capture answers on newsprint for future sessions:

- If our mission is to do all we can to make, form, and shape others into disciples of Jesus Christ for the transformation of the world, how is our congregation actively engaged in making disciples?

- Where do you see Christ working through our church?

- Do the folks who make up our congregation understand what it means to be disciples?

- How do we move our congregation to have a better understanding of what it means to be a disciple? (This question should generate lots of thoughts and ideas).

Closing

State together the mission of the church:

To make disciples of Jesus Christ for the transformation of the world.

Read or have read Matthew 28:16-20 again.

Ask individuals to name one thing they have learned or have a new understanding about as a result of this session.

Close in prayer, in whatever way seems appropriate, and read this benediction together:

*May the Lord make your love increase and overflow for each other and
for everyone else, just as ours does for you.*

(1 Thessalonians 3:12, NIV)

Ask the team members to be in prayer about the mission and to ask their prayer partners for special prayers as you continue. Hand out Individual Preparation for Step 4, and remind them to study it before the next session.

 LEADER/FACILITATOR: Keep the prayer strategy moving forward. Collect the names of the prayer partners your team members have chosen, and remind the team to ask their prayer partners to cover them in prayer. Be aware that the next step may spark some conflict as the participants struggle with the meaning of disciple. If you have not worked with conflict resolution, check justpeaceumc.org, a United Methodist Center for Mediation and Conflict Transformation.

 TEAM: Continue to pray as you prepare for the next session, allowing God to work through you. Also, begin to be alert to persons in the congregation who are searching to follow Christ in new and different ways. Consider leading Discovery Activity 1 and the Bible Study for Step 3 for other groups in the church.

 PASTOR: Take advantage of opportunities to preach on the mission of your church to motivate, inspire, and stir the people. Cast a vision for disciple formation through sermons, newsletters, teaching opportunities—any means to help the church see what it can look like to have a disciple formation process that is unique to your context. Consider preaching on Matthew 28:16-20 as well as other texts around the theme of discipleship (Micah 6:8, Galatians 5:22-23, Nicodemus, the woman at the well, Peter, Saul/Paul, and so on).

 INVITING THE CONGREGATION: Request that the congregation read and reflect on Matthew 28:16-20. Offer to lead Bible study for groups and meetings. See the instruction above for Team.

 CHECK YOUR BEARINGS: Is the team committed to the concept that the most important role for your congregation is to make disciples for Jesus Christ? Did some ideas come from the team about ways to help the entire congregation have this same commitment?

Bible Study for Step 3

Now the eleven disciples went to Galilee, to the mountain where Jesus told them to go. When they saw him, they worshipped him, but some doubted. Jesus came near and spoke to them, "I've received all authority in heaven and on earth. Therefore, go and make disciples of all nations, baptizing them in the name of the Father and of the Son and of the Holy Spirit, teaching them to obey everything that I've commanded you. Look, I myself will be with you every day until the end of this present age."

(Matthew 28:16-20, CEB)

- What do you think of when you read these words in verse 19, "Go and make disciples of all nations"?

- Did you realize you were involved in making a new disciple of Christ in the situations you mentioned in our earlier activity? What was your part in that? What was the part of the Holy Spirit in it?

- What are some ways a person grows closer to Christ?

   He replied, "You must love the Lord your God with all your heart, with all your being, and with all your mind. This is the first and greatest commandment. And the second is like it: You must love your neighbor as you love yourself. All the Law and the Prophets depend on these two commands."

(Matthew 22:37-40, CEB)

- How do you practice the love of God and neighbor in your daily life?

- Can you name ways you've grown deeper?

- What are specific things that have helped you grow deeper along the way (individuals, ministries of your church, etc.)?

- How is growing deeper in love of God and neighbor related to discipleship?

John and Charles Wesley, founders of the Methodist movement, believed that growing deeper (more perfect) in love of God and neighbor was the purpose of discipleship. They taught that it is a lifelong journey.

- Read again the two passages. How do they connect or relate to one another?

Individual Preparation

Read this ahead of time, and bring it with you to our Step 4 meeting.

Centering Prayer

God of unity and love, we thank you for your guidance. As we work to gain a common understanding of a disciple, and as we seek to define spiritual practices, keep us focused on you. May you unite this congregation so that we may embrace for ourselves who you call us to be. We pray in the name of Christ, who unites us in one body. Amen.

Scripture

Jesus' eleven disciples went to a mountain in Galilee, where Jesus had told them to meet him. They saw him and worshiped him, but some of them doubted. Jesus came to them and said: I have been given all authority in heaven and on earth! Go to the people of all nations and make them my disciples. Baptize them in the name of the Father, the Son, and the Holy Spirit, and teach them to do everything I have told you. I will be with you always, even until the end of the world.

(Matthew 28:16-20, CEV)

Reflection

When we next meet, we will work on a description of a disciple. Some people who have been Christians for a long time will say, "Everybody knows what a disciple is! We don't need to define it!" But much that goes on in our churches does not flow out of a desire for disciple making. If we understand our mission to be about making disciples, we need to be clear what a disciple is. The task of creating a common description of disciple for our congregation can be helpful, informative, and inspiring. As the congregation begins to gain consensus around a description of disciple, it will help them understand more clearly what the church is trying to "produce" as the congregation fulfills the mission to make disciples.

Read one or more of these passages, reflecting on what it means to be a disciple:

- Matthew 8:5-13 (the centurion, a man who had absolute confidence in the authority of Jesus)

- Acts 9:19b-22 (Saul, whose mission was redefined by Christ)

- Acts 8:26-39 (the Ethiopian eunuch, who eagerly desired to be baptized so that he might be identified as a disciple)

- Matthew 9:35–10:8 (Jesus asking the disciples to pray for workers, then sending them out to be the workers)

- John 4:1-30 (the woman at the well)

- Acts 20:1-6 (part of Paul's missionary travels)

- Acts 2:14-42 (Peter's powerful sermon on the day of Pentecost, and the subsequent addition of 3,000 persons into the faith)

- John 9 (the man born blind, who was healed by Jesus)

- Philippians 2 (having the mind of Christ in humility)

Reflect on these Bible passages and write down your thoughts:

- How would you describe a disciple of Jesus Christ?

- Do you see yourself as being one? Why or why not?

- What are the basic practices that you do as a disciple?

What's the mission of the church again? Yes, you've heard it over and over again. But once more:

The mission of the congregation is to make disciples of Jesus Christ for the transformation of the world.

So what is a disciple?

If the church is supposed to make disciples, then just what is a disciple?

In the Great Commission, Matthew 28:16-20, the risen Christ tells the apostles to go into the world to make disciples. But that doesn't tell us what a disciple is.

Let's put this idea another way:

- If our job is to make disciples, how do we know when we've accomplished that task?

- How do we know if we've "made" a disciple?

- What does a disciple look like? Act like?

- What does a disciple do that is different from what everyone else does?

- And do we make a disciple like we make a cake or a birdhouse? "There. It's finished. Now let's do something else."

Here's an interesting thought: Once a disciple, always a disciple. True? Let's think about that one.

The place to start, of course, is with the Scriptures. The Bible gives us clues and insights that we want to plumb in order to understand as profoundly as possible just what a disciple is. But simply reading about the disciples—or the apostles—in the New Testament doesn't give us a full understanding of what a disciple is today.

According to the Gospels, Jesus had many disciples. These included men and women, young people and old, children and youth, Jews and Gentiles, rich and poor, city dwellers and country folk, the very religious and the slightly religious. What bound them together, what made them as one, was their allegiance to Jesus.

Let's put that another way: Perhaps the only common characteristic that all the disciples of Jesus shared was that they all believed in Jesus (at least, most of the time), in what he was doing, and in what he was teaching as he roamed the Holy Land. All those disciples of Jesus believed in what Jesus was teaching; but like you and me, not all of them understood all that Jesus was teaching. But, again like you and me, all were struck by the winsomeness of his words and all were eager to see what he would say and do next.

> ➧ So, knowing what Jesus was teaching must be an important part of making a disciple.

Nowhere in the Bible do we read about Jesus saying that we must "be saved" or "give our heart to Jesus" in order to be a disciple. Although these concepts are rich in tradition and based in Scripture, you and I cannot define for someone else how she or he will make a commitment to follow Jesus Christ. That commitment may come in a blinding flash, as it did to Paul on the road to Damascus. Or it may come slowly over time, as it did to the apostles Thomas and Peter or as Timothy learned about God's love from his mother and grandmother. It may come in "fits and starts" as it did to John Wesley, one of the founders of the Methodist movement.

You see, because each of us is an individual, we will respond to Jesus Christ in our own individual ways. We cannot evaluate another's decision to follow Jesus, especially if we judge it alongside our decision to follow Jesus. The Gospels are rich in stories of how different persons responded to Jesus, but each responded in his or her own unique way.

> ➧ So, no *one* way of becoming a disciple is more important than another.

And, just as we cannot dictate how another will make a commitment to Jesus Christ, neither can we dictate the form or the living out of that commitment. What's that mean? Simply this:

Apostles or Disciples

Let's clear up a bit of technical language here. Jesus chose twelve persons to be apostles. The term, *apostles*, refers to these twelve, even though the lists of the names of these twelve are not the same in all the versions of the gospel. You can read about Jesus' naming the apostles in Matthew 10:1-4; Mark 3:13-19a; and Luke 6:12-16. But before each of these twelve was selected as an apostle, that person was a disciple. In other words, an apostle is not a different order or level of disciple. The word *apostle* simply refers to the twelve who formed the immediate and intimate group around Jesus throughout his ministry. So what we are describing in this step are not the twelve apostles— but disciples.

39

Disciples of Jesus Christ are called by Christ to undertake a bewildering variety of tasks.

God does not call all disciples to be choir members or teachers or preachers or trustees or any other one or two things. God *does* call all disciples to a careful and prayerful discernment—that means discovery—of God's call on their lives through Jesus Christ.

God also calls us to continue to grow as disciples. We cannot say, "Now I'm a disciple and I no longer need to stretch my spirituality." We must be intentional in our growing throughout our lives. And so we must purposefully provide a variety of opportunities in the church for continual growth and service. Even a knitting group, or a book club, or those who prepare mid-week suppers, or a nursery worker, or a children's or youth group must understand where they fit as disciples, carrying out God's call.

What's the upshot of all of this? Your neighbor is no less a disciple of Jesus Christ than you are just because he or she does not live out his or her discipleship the same way you do! The common denominator is that all disciples do what they do out of a **commitment** to Jesus Christ.

All of the time? Of course not. Disciples stumble and fall. (An old Methodist word, "backslide," captures that experience.) But disciples experience forgiveness through the grace of God. (The word, "grace" can be defined as an "I love you anyway" love.) People who stumble receive grace to pick themselves up, dust themselves off, and begin again to live as forgiven people. To live as a forgiven person is to respond to God's grace by actively loving what God loves. What is that? "That" is our sisters and brothers next door and around the world. We love because God first loved us through Christ.

Shorthand? Disciples are people who demonstrate their love of and response to Christ by loving one another in word, in deed, in prayer, and in every other possible way. Want to add something like that to your list of characteristics of a disciple?

Wow! These insights only make the mission of disciple-making more difficult, don't they? If we could say all disciples experience a call to discipleship in this way or that way and all disciples do this or that in response to that call, the task would be easier. But that simply is not the case. This may make our challenge of making disciples a bit more difficult, but the results will be infinitely richer for it!

Now, look at the description you wrote for a disciple at the beginning of this handout. What would you add or take away? How would you change it? Remember, we're not looking for a dictionary definition, but a working one.

May the Lord make your love increase and overflow for each other
and for everyone else, just as ours does for you.
(1 Thessalonians 3:12, NIV)

40

Step 4

FINDING TRUE NORTH

What's a Disciple?

The team has come together and embraced disciple making as your mission. The goal of this step is to discover and express a description of the word disciple, including a list of what disciples do. Some communal practices will be unique to the context of your local church.

God of unity and love,

We thank you for your guidance.

As we work to gain a common understanding of a disciple,

and as we seek to define spiritual practices, keep us focused on you.

May you unite this congregation so that we may embrace for ourselves

who you call us to be.

We pray in the name of Christ, who unites us in one body.

Amen.

Step 4 at a Glance

Goals

- To describe a disciple.

- To list the spiritual practices of a disciple.

- To identify ways to lead the congregation to describe a disciple.

- To begin to discover how your congregation can fulfill the mission of the church, which is to make disciples for Jesus Christ for the transformation of the world.

Possible Format

- Worship

- Discovery Activity 1

- Bible Study

- Group Reflection on Individual Preparation

- Discovery Activity 2

- Closing

Several Sessions

It may take several sessions to cover the material in this step, especially if the team decides to lead the activities with other groups in the congregation. You will need ample time for the Discovery Activities and Bible Study.

Preparation

- Place a candle and matches on the table. (Or use a battery-operated candle.)

- Make copies of Individual Preparation for the next session and the Bible study for this session.

- Provide sticky-note papers and pencils or pens. Also provide 3 x 5 cards for team members to write the agreed upon definition of a disciple, as suggested in the closing prayer time.

- Using a whiteboard or a long paper, write the heading: A disciple of Jesus Christ is a person who...

- If possible, become familiar with John Wesley's definition of disciple in his sermon "A More Excellent Way." The sermon is available on several websites.

Worship

- Light the candle and remind them of its meaning and that anyone may blow it out and relight it if at some time during your time together you do not act or speak as you would if Christ were physically here with you.

- State together the mission of the church:

    To make disciples of Jesus Christ for the transformation of the world.

- Read the centering prayer from the Individual Preparation page for this session.

- Read together Matthew 28:16-20, using the version printed on their handout.

- Ask where they have seen God at work in their lives or in the life of the church since last you met.

- Pray a prayer similar to this: Our God, we thank you for the many times you have been evident in our lives recently. We ask that you be with us today as we center on just what it means to be a disciple of Christ. Amen.

Discovery Activity 1

- Pass out sticky notes and pencils or pens.

- Ask individuals, in total silence, to write one word or short phrase on each sticky note that describes a "disciple." They can remember the Scripture that they just read together and the ideas they had during preparation. And they can think about a person they consider a disciple and list words that describe the person, rather than focusing on a dictionary definition of a disciple. (This task should take several minutes.)

- Place these sticky notes on a wall under a sentence stem like "A disciple of Jesus Christ is a person who . . ."

- Continuing in silence, ask people to read the notes and begin to cluster these notes that seem similar. Some categories will emerge such as beliefs, actions, relationships, practices, and so on.

Bible Study

Pass out the Bible Study for Step 4 and work through it together.

Group Reflection on Individual Preparation

Discuss thoughts about the Individual Preparation for Step 4.

Working together as a team, begin to construct one or two sentences describing a disciple. Start with "A disciple is . . . " Test your definition against the mission of the church, against Matthew 28:19-20, and against our Wesleyan theology. (A good source for understanding John Wesley's definition of "disciple" is his sermon "A More Excellent Way.")

Work with your material until there is consensus on the team with the description.

Your short definition may not capture everything, so for future sessions make a list of practices of a disciple.

Discovery Activity 2

Refer to the information with the icons at the end of this session. Explain to the team that each step includes both individual learning and responsibility to lead the congregation. Review the Team and the Inviting the Congregation sections. Together list ways to fulfill these roles; then develop a plan for inviting the congregation on the journey of intentional disciple formation.

Closing

State together the mission of the church:

To make disciples of Jesus Christ for the transformation of the world.

Read or have read Matthew 28:16-20 again.

Ask: *How will the decisions made during this step "make disciples for Jesus Christ for the transformation of the world"?*

Hand out 3 x 5 cards; invite the team members to write your description of a disciple on their card and put it in a place where they can see it daily. Suggest that they ask God to show them, every day, ways that they need to grow as a disciple.

Close in prayer, in whatever way seems appropriate, and read this benediction together:

May the Lord make your love increase and overflow for each other
and for everyone else, just as ours does for you.

(1 Thessalonians 3:12, NIV)

Ask the team members to be in prayer about the mission and to ask their prayer partners for special prayers as you continue. Hand out Individual Preparation for Step 5 and remind them to study it before the next session.

LEADER/FACILITATOR: Look ahead to Step 5 because it will take a longer time frame or perhaps two sessions. Plan with your group so that you can have additional time. Continue to pray for the team and the church members. Find ways to share the description of a disciple with the total congregation. Help people understand that this is a working description, which can be changed as needed. Invite feedback from the congregation.

TEAM: Ask for input from your congregation on describing a disciple, including a list of spiritual practices of a disciple. Find additional ways to share with other members of the congregation what you're learning about a disciple. Include this conversation, as appropriate, in small groups that you're a part of.

PASTOR: As spiritual leader of the congregation, be fully engaged in the development of the description of a disciple and share it through sermons, newsletters, Christian conferencing, and the other communication venues of your congregation.

INVITING THE CONGREGATION: Publish your working description of a disciple, and ask the congregation to put it in a place where they can see it daily. Suggest that they ask God to show them, every day, ways they need to grow as a disciple. In this way, your congregation will begin to build ownership of the description. Stress that it is in development, and that they can continue to give input. In one small congregation the team led Discovery Activity 1 during Sunday worship, engaging everyone in describing a disciple.

CHECK YOUR BEARINGS: Are there differences of opinion and interpretation cropping up? The reason for developing a "church-owned" description is precisely because among people in churches there are different viewpoints and ideas about what a disciple is. Have you charged persons on the team with being aware of the emotional climate, keeping eyes, ears, and heart tuned to what people are saying behind closed doors? Are your communication lines open and clear? Are you saying things multiple times in several different ways?

Bible Study for Step 4

All the Lord's followers often met together, and they shared everything they had. They would sell their property and possessions and give the money to whoever needed it. Day after day they met together in the temple. They broke bread together in different homes and shared their food happily and freely, while praising God. Everyone liked them, and each day the Lord added to their group others who were being saved.

(Acts 2:44-47, CEV)

• Think of someone in your past who did acts that seem typical of a disciple.

• How did that person influence your life?

• In the Scripture how did Jesus' followers act toward each other?

• What seemed to help the growth of the group of disciples?

• How is our church congregation today like the one mentioned in Acts?

• How could we be more like these disciples?

Individual Preparation

Read this ahead of time, and bring it with you to our Step 5 meeting.

Centering Prayer

Holy and wondrous God, you were present and active in the world since the beginning of time, and we have much to learn from your activity throughout the span of life. As we learn, work, and grow together, show us how we can learn from the faithful who have gone before us, and show us how to learn from those who are making disciples now. May the principles that guided them guide us as we seek to make disciples; and in all things, God, keep our eyes focused on the teachings and actions of Jesus, in whose name we pray. Amen.

Scripture

You Gentiles are no longer strangers and foreigners. You are citizens with everyone else who belongs to the family of God. You are like a building with the apostles and prophets as the foundation and with Christ as the most important stone. Christ is the one who holds the building together and makes it grow into a holy temple for the Lord. And you are part of that building Christ has built as a place for God's own Spirit to live.

(Ephesians 2:19-22, CEV)

Let the wonderful kindness and the understanding that come from our Lord and Savior Jesus Christ help you to keep on growing. Praise Jesus now and forever! Amen

(2 Peter 3:18, CEV)

Reflection

OK. What's the mission of the church again?

To make disciples of Jesus Christ for the transformation of the world.

So how does a congregation focus its energies toward that mission? You gotta wanna. Historically, the church has created systems to meet the needs of the moment in their efforts to make disciples. What makes those systems effective in the mission? Well, they follow certain principles. You will soon have a chance to look at your own setting to assess how we're doing in disciple making. But first we'll look at some examples and see what principles we can learn about how to effectively make disciples.

> Congregations are made up of people who are on this journey together but are at different levels of faith formation.

Discipleship is a process. The apostle John (John 1:16) tells us that we receive grace upon grace, which John Wesley felt reflected a process. Discipleship requires forward movement. Understanding faith as a continuous journey can be a daunting task for some people. We live in an age of instant gratification. When we want something we go out and buy it. We'd rather buy our bread at the store than make it at home. We buy on credit instead of saving up to purchase something. But the completion of a disciple isn't done instantly. It is a lifetime process.

If you were to plot your faith journey through your lifetime, it would probably have ups and downs, showing high points and low points in your relationship with God. Here is one person's faith-line:

Plot Your Faith Line

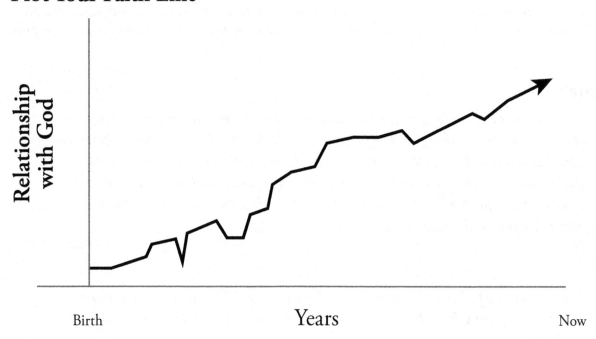

For some people, there is a specific, identifiable time of commitment to Christian living. John Wesley called this "new birth." Today, people might refer to "being saved" or "giving my heart to Jesus."

Some other people cannot remember a time when they were not Christian. Others describe a relationship with God that has grown slowly over time. Many people make re-commitments to Christian living throughout their life.

What's your experience? **Plot your faith-line here** as you look back on your life with God.

Birth　　　　　　　　　　　　Years　　　　　　　　　　Now

Notice when you have felt especially close to God and remember what was happening in your life. What influenced you during high moments and in low times? Does your faith-line show a general upward trend?

Look at your faith-line again. Mark your earliest awareness of God. Mark the first time you committed to follow Christ. Can you identify the times you had a deeper understanding of God and of the commitments of Christian living?

While your faith-line is uniquely your own, it's important to note that people continue to grow spiritually from birth throughout adulthood. A faith-line is a reflection of your relationship with God, not your beliefs. We expect each person's relationship with God to grow, even as beliefs may change. As you understand your own faith development, you begin to appreciate the many ways people grow. Christians have noticed that people have a pattern of growing in faith that has some similarities. Therefore, it is important that our team develop a set of markers or stages for the journey in order to develop an intentional faith development plan for our congregation. Such markers allow people associated with your congregation to see stages of personal growth, as well as a goal toward which they can work.

Just as an oak is an oak, whether a seedling or a hundred-year-old giant, so we all have a faith and need affirmation and support in that faith, no matter what stage we function from. Part of our job as a team is to provide opportunities for those in our congregation to continue to grow in all levels and not become stuck at one stage or another.

May the Lord make your love increase and overflow for each other
and for everyone else, just as ours does for you.
(1 Thessalonians 3:12, NIV)

Step 5

STUDYING THE MAPS

Looking Around

You have started to describe what it means to be a disciple in your particular local church context, and the team is beginning to understand the importance of life-long discipleship. In this step, you will look at several examples of disciple forming processes (historical and current). Remember that your system of growing disciples must be intentional and uniquely developed for your context.

Holy and wondrous God,

you were present and active in the world since the beginning of time,

and we have much to learn from your activity throughout the span of life. As we learn,

work, and grow together, show us how we can learn from the faithful who have gone

before us, and show us how to learn from those who are making disciples now. May

the principles that guided them guide us as we seek to make disciples;

and in all things, God, keep our eyes focused on the teachings and actions of Jesus,

in whose name we pray. Amen.

Step 5 at a Glance

Goals

- To study and understand disciple formation according to John Wesley and how it relates to the Wesleyan understanding of grace.

- To become familiar with an intentional design for helping all people grow in discipleship.

- To examine some disciple formation systems developed by other congregations.

- To begin a list of essential components to have as part of your church's disciple formation process. The team will continue to develop this list over several steps.

Possible Format

- Worship

- Discovery Activity 1

- Bible Study

- Discovery Activity 2

- Discovery Activity 3

- Closing

> ### Multiple-Sessions Plan
>
> This step may take multiple sessions to complete. Consider one session for the first two goals and another session for the next two goals.
>
> You may want to break for a second session between Discovery Activity 2 and 3.

Preparation

- Place a candle and matches on the table. (Or use a battery-operated candle.)

- Make copies of the three handouts for the Discovery Activities, the Individual Preparation for the next session, and the Bible study for this session.

- Provide newsprint and markers

 INVITING THE CONGREGATION: At this stage, you may have a plan for teaching others in your congregation what you are learning about discipleship. Remind the congregation of the mission of the church and your vision of an intentional plan for growing in faith and discipleship. Taking time to bring others on board now is important. The hearts and minds of people and the mission are worth this careful attention.

 YOUR CHURCH: If you are a small church, you may want to use the study information with the whole adult congregation.

Worship

- Light the candle and remind them of its meaning and that anyone may blow it out and relight it if at some time during your time together you do not act or speak as you would if Christ were physically here with you.

- State together the mission of the church:

    To make disciples of Jesus Christ for the transformation of the world.

- Read the centering prayer from the Individual Preparation together, or have someone read it while the group meditates.

- Ask where they have seen God at work in their lives or in the life of the church since last you met.

- Read together Ephesians 2:19-22 and 2 Peter 3:18 on the Individual Preparation handout.

- Pray a prayer similar to this: Our God, our Leader, be with us now as we look at people and churches who have struggled to fulfill the mission of making disciples. Keep us open to all possibilities, not just accepting what someone else has done. We know that we are a unique gathering of your people, and we want to follow your leading. Amen.

Discovery Activity 1

- Ask people to refer to their preparation for this step, especially the faith-line they created. Invite them to share a new insight about their own faith development.

- Relate the information from the sidebar about the Wesleyan understanding of discipleship (Lifelong Journey). As a visual aid, give participants Handout 5A.

- Ask members to tell how they have experienced prevenient, justifying, and sanctifying grace.

Lifelong Journey

John Wesley understood discipleship as a lifelong journey where we develop in different stages—hopefully growing deeper and deeper in our love of God and neighbor.

The Wesley brothers, John and Charles, who launched the Methodist movement, developed an understanding that God works with us throughout our lives. For John Wesley, salvation was not something only in the future, after death. He believed it was also a present reality grounded in the grace of God.

Steve Manskar in his book, **Accountable Discipleship**, describes Wesley's understanding of salvation as "to be set free from sin (separation and alienation from God), to be restored to a right relationship with God, and to have the brokenness of your heart and life restored to wholeness. All this has been done for you by God in Jesus Christ" (page 63).

Charles Wesley expressed the same ideas through many hymns that are in **The United Methodist Hymnal**, for example, "Love Divine, All Loves Excelling" (#384). Verse 4 has the phrase, "changed from glory into glory, till in heaven we take our place."

Lifelong Grace

John Wesley believed Christians are on a lifelong spiritual pilgrimage, and our growth in discipleship parallels God's gift of grace.

The Wesleyan path of growth, called "the way of salvation" or "going toward perfection" is marked by various types of grace. "Grace" is a term to describe God's love for us, who are God's human creatures. Here is a diagram of Wesley's understanding of grace throughout our faith journey:

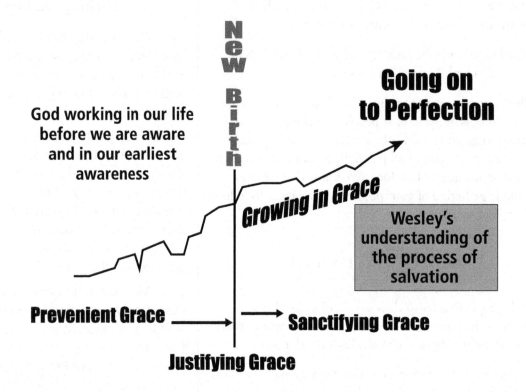

Prevenient Grace: Wesley saw that this was given to all persons, and that it even works in their lives before they encounter Christ.

Justifying Grace: When people are moved to repent of their sin and commit to following Jesus, they experience justifying grace, assuring them of God's presence in their lives and giving them new life in Christ.

Sanctifying Grace: Wesley saw this as the grace that moves people onward toward Christian perfection.

Bible Study

Pass out the Bible Study for Step 5 and work through it together.

Discovery Activity 2

- Continue to help the team know more about their Wesleyan heritage and how it plays into the task at hand. Tell the group that the Wesleys understood that people are at various places on their faith journey and the community must provide different experiences and levels of support for people to grow as disciples. So during his lifetime, John Wesley and the Methodist leaders developed a series of opportunities for people to come and grow in faith.

- Go over The Wesleyan Way (Handout 5B) with the team so they can see Wesley's system of intentional opportunities for people at each stage of their faith journey.

- Use the information in the sidebar (Living in Grace) to further illustrate the Wesleyan approach.

- Point out to the group that growing in faith, sanctification, is not nearly as linear and neat as these diagrams would indicate. Life is "messy" and our faith journeys are often messy, as well. There are times when we feel very close to God and can see the results of God working in our lives to help us grow. At other times we may feel further apart from God and don't see any growth or progress. But over time, as we practice spiritual disciplines, study, worship and continue to seek God, God will work in our lives and we will mature into the persons we are created to be.

- Ask team members how they have experienced a class or experience as a stepping-stone in their faith life.

- Ask how this information connects with life in your congregation. What might develop from your work to build an intentional system in your congregation?

Living in Grace

All of the opportunities in Wesley's system for faith formation were designed to meet people where they were and lead them into deeper and deeper experiences of God and help them along the way of salvation toward Christian perfection.

We can apply Wesley's approach to our congregations today—taking seriously the need for different kinds of experiences and growth opportunities for persons at different times on their faith journey. There are many different ways to name stages of faith. One way to describe a faith-life uses the image of a house:

Prevenient grace brings us to the porch and gets us ready to receive God's grace and forgiveness. Justifying grace opens the door and helps us walk into a right relationship with God. Sanctifying grace helps us to live in the house, growing more and more into the likeness of Christ.

The Wesleyan Way

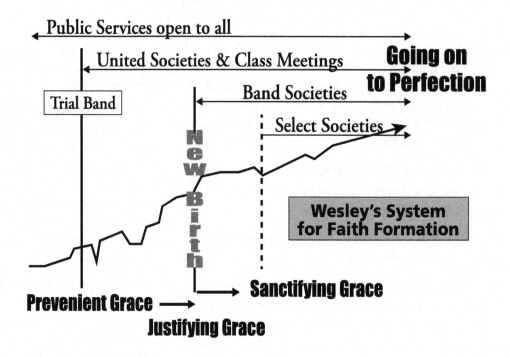

First, **public services**—open to all—were held (Prevenient Grace). Wesley did not wait for people to come to a church building. He went out and preached in the fields to whoever would listen. For people not yet ready to commit but who wanted to know more, he organized **trial bands**. These were opportunities for individuals to explore the Christian faith and decide if they were serious about joining a society.

Then if persons wished to grow in their faith ("flee from the wrath to come"), he encouraged participation in societies and class meetings. He understood people needed structure for their emerging faith to grow and mature. The larger **societies** were a place where they could find instruction in the basics of Christian faith and receive the support and accountability they needed as they expressed their desires for God and finding a way to live as a disciple. Wesley also ordered the Methodist societies into smaller class meetings under the leadership of lay class-leaders, who provided the pastoral care and guidance needed to nurture the people as they grew in their faith.

Band societies were for individuals who had made a decision to follow Christ and had an experience of new birth (Justifying Grace). There they focused on practicing the means of grace and growing deeper in Christian discipleship.

Select societies were for those who were ready to move on to an even deeper faith and possible leadership in the societies and class meetings (Sanctifying Grace). The emphasis here was on loving God and neighbor and living a life of service.

Discovery Activity 3

- Make a beginning list of principles from our Wesleyan heritage that you want to include in your plan for intentional disciple formation.

- Using the examples below, add to your list of principles. Look at these examples of contemporary models of a discipleship system from several congregations. They have taken seriously the idea of different stages during the disciple formation and created something that fits their particular context. Read aloud each example. After each, identify and list principles:

  ○ Brentwood United Methodist Church in Brentwood, Tennessee, seeks to engage people in a lifelong process of discipleship, using river imagery as a means to mark points along a spiritual journey. Workshops, classes, and various ministry opportunities are offered at each stage to help move individuals further along. Stages identified are "Checking out the Scene," "Stepping in the Water," "Riding the Rapids," "Diving Deeper," and "Going Fishing."

  ○ Murphysboro United Methodist Church in Murphysboro, Illinois, invites people to join them in the "greatest journey of your life," a journey of discipleship, as they endeavor to become a community of deeply committed Christians. Using a trail imagery, they identify the stages as "At the Trailhead," "On the Path," "At the Lookout," "Off the Path," and "On the Cliffs."

  ○ Benton First United Methodist in Benton, Kentucky, organizes various classes and experiences around similar path imagery. Different stages are described as "Getting Your Bearings," "Finding a Path," "On an Adventure," "Deeper Exploration," Being a "Discipling Guide," and "Quest for Holiness."

  ○ Another congregation chose to use the following:

    Exploring Christ   "I believe in God, but I am not sure about Christ"

    Growing in Christ   "I believe in Jesus and I am working on what that means"

    Close to Christ   "I feel really close to Christ and depend on him daily"

    Christ-Centered   "My relationship with Jesus is the most important thing in my life"

- Handout 5C shows the focus of a congregation that has a strong outreach to unchurched and dechurched people. In their book, *Deepening Your Effectiveness: Restructuring the Local Church for Life Transformation* (Discipleship Resources, 2006). Dan Glover and Claudia Lavy use a metaphor of stepping into the ocean. Their ocean stages are "Life on the Beach," "Life on the Shoreline," "Life in the Waves," "Life When Your Feet Come Off the Bottom," "Life Beyond the Breakers," and "Life in the Deep."

(Handout 5C)

An Example

Many people are **outside the influence of the church**. They do not even know they are seeking God, or they are looking elsewhere for meaning in their life. But God, through prevenient grace, is reaching out to them. Our task as a congregation is to offer radical hospitality—to meet them wherever they are and model what it means to be a loving disciple of Jesus Christ.

Other persons are **cautious**, perhaps suspicious of the church or uncomfortable and unsure about the Christian faith. They may be reluctant to visit a church. We can get to know their name, develop a relationship with them and introduce them to others who are a part of a Christian community.

Some people are **curious** about the Christian faith and want to know more. They may not have engaged with a formal group of Christians and are not convinced that the Christian life is for them. Our role here is to create opportunities to satisfy their curiosity and to relate them to other Christians in non-threatening ways. Short-term service opportunities or classes about basic beliefs of the faith might be options here.

Others have made a **commitment** to a group or congregation but not yet to a personal relationship with Christ. They are not yet disciplined in growing in their faith. Opportunities here might include longer-term studies, ministry through service, and opportunities to make a decision for Christ.

Professing Christians have committed to having Christ at the center of life. They are aware of God's presence and ready to go deeper in faith. Congregations can offer people at this stage an emphasis on living as members of the body of Christ and opportunities to focus on the disciplines of the faith.

Individuals at the **inviting** stage are deeply committed to God and the Christian faith. They seek to help others into discipleship and focus on living their faith in the world. Congregations can support people at this stage by providing advanced leadership training, sharing strategies for reaching others, and offering significant leadership roles to them.

• Review the list you have been making. What principles have you identified? Make the point that these various examples show that Wesley's approach can apply to our congregations today.

• Discuss the idea of different stages of faith and talk about how you might describe them for your congregation. In the next step you will decide the stages appropriate for your congregation.

Closing

State together the mission of the church:

To make disciples of Jesus Christ for the transformation of the world.

• How will the decisions made during this step help fulfill that mission?

Read or have read Ephesians 2:19-22 again.

Close in prayer, in whatever way seems appropriate, and read this benediction together:

May the Lord make your love increase and overflow for each other
and for everyone else, just as ours does for you.

(1 Thessalonians 3:12, NIV)

Ask the team members to be in prayer about the mission and to ask their prayer partners for special prayers. Hand out Individual Preparation for Step 6 and remind them to study it before the next session.

 LEADER/FACILITATOR: Begin to collect ideas for the next meeting; come with a list of the church's activities and ministries. Step 6 may take a little more preparation than usual.

 TEAM: Continue to reflect on the various models of discipleship you learned about in the session. Also, share some of these thoughts with persons in the congregation.

 PASTOR: Use a sermon to teach the congregation about Wesley's system, looking at how it works in today's context. Continue to support the team as they engage in study and dialogue.

 INVITING THE CONGREGATION: Look for ways to engage the congregation in the suggested Bible studies, remembering that Bible study is not only for studying the Bible but also for helping to form groups.

 CHECK YOUR BEARINGS: Are there persons in the congregation who do not understand what the team is trying to do? How can you help them recognize that these meetings are more than another gathering? Are you encouraging the congregation to pray for the work of the team?

Bible Study for Step 5

Read John 1:14-18 in various translations, including this one:

And the Word became flesh and lived among us, and we have seen his glory, the glory as of a father's only son, full of grace and truth. (John testified to him and cried out, "This was he of whom I said, 'He who comes after me ranks ahead of me because he was before me.'") From his fullness we have all received, grace upon grace. The law indeed was given through Moses; grace and truth came through Jesus Christ. No one has ever seen God. It is God the only Son, who is close to the Father's heart, who has made him known.

(John 1:14-18, NRSV)

- From the fullness of the Word become flesh, we have received "grace upon grace." What evidence do you have that God has bestowed prevenient, justifying, and sanctifying grace on you?

- We are recipients of the Word's fullness. How do you recognize the movement of the Word in your life? in the life of the congregation?

- Where have you seen the congregation experience "grace upon grace," and what has been the effect of grace on the congregation?

- "Grace upon grace" implies continual growth. How does the image of us receiving "grace upon grace" relate to disciple formation?

Individual Preparation

Read this ahead of time, and bring it with you to our Step 6 meeting.

Centering Prayer

Ever-faithful God, we thank you for always being present with us. We praise you for your work in the early church, giving us an example of how to form and shape disciples. If our work becomes hard, God, call us back to you, so that we might refocus on who we are, and whose we are. By your Spirit, may you shape and mold us into faithful disciples of Jesus Christ. Amen.

What is the mission of the local church again?

The mission of the church is to make disciples of Jesus Christ for the transformation of the world.

We have struggled with a working description of a disciple—just what a disciple of Jesus Christ is and what a disciple does. Keep in mind that our description of a disciple is "open"—that means we can change, adapt, adjust, and refine that description as we continue developing our approach to disciple formation. Just as persons are always changing, so the functional definition of a disciple of Jesus Christ is always changing. But those changes are changes in emphasis; they are not changes in fundamental and basic concepts.

Think of the description of a disciple of Jesus Christ as a kaleidoscope. You look through a kaleidoscope and twist it to see wonderful designs and shapes. Remember that although you see different designs and shapes through the kaleidoscope, it is the same bits of colored glass that make all those shapes and designs. So it is with a description of a disciple.

We have looked at a disciple formation system from our Wesleyan heritage and examples from contemporary congregations of all sizes. The team is beginning to dream about our own congregation full of Christian disciples. What would our congregation look like if everyone were engaged in a disciple formation process?

As we have worked together as a team, has a metaphor begun to form in your mind? Metaphors provide visual, mental, and emotional stimuli, or guides for the discipleship journey Have you heard others discuss metaphors we might use? In Step 5, we saw how congregations have used the image of a river or a path to symbolize their disciple formation system. Some other metaphors are a tree (beginning with a seedling, and using growth stages or even tree branches), rings of a cross cut tree trunk, a flower, a web, a graph, a waterfall, keys to treasure boxes, kites of varying heights and such.

> ## Unchanging— Yet Changing
> The fundamental characteristics of what a disciple is and what a disciple does are unchanging, but the arrangements and concentration of those characteristics may change over a lifetime and in a particular context.

• As you prepare for Step 6, make notes or draw an image that might be a metaphor for your congregation's disciple formation. Be creative and think outside the box!

• Your congregation is already doing a lot. Take several minutes to list everything you can think of that happens at your church now. Who comes to the church and for what purpose? What do members do in the community in the name of your congregation? What events, activities and meetings happen? List as many things as you can think of that your church does. Be sure to bring the list to our next meeting.

May the Lord make your love increase and overflow for each other
and for everyone else, just as ours does for you.
(1 Thessalonians 3:12, NIV)

Step 6

CHECKING OUR BEARINGS

What Are We Doing?

The team has come to an understanding of the mission of the church and wrestled with just what it means to be a disciple. You have also looked at John Wesley's system for forming disciples and some contemporary disciple-formation approaches. In this step you will examine the current reality of disciple making in your congregation, and begin to create a framework for an intentional plan to invite everyone to grow as Christian disciples.

Ever-faithful God,

We thank you for always being present with us. We praise you for your work

in the early church, giving us an example of how to form and shape disciples. If our work

becomes hard, God, call us back to you, so that we might refocus on who we are,

and Whose we are.

By your Spirit, may you shape and mold us into faithful disciples

of Jesus Christ. Amen.

Step 6 at a Glance

Goals

- To identify all the ministry activities in your church.

- To determine if, and how, each one contributes to making disciples for Jesus Christ.

- To begin building a framework for an intentional discipleship system.

Possible Format

- Worship

- Discovery Activity 1

- Bible Study

- Discovery Activity 2

- Discovery Activity 3

- Closing

Preparation

- Place a candle and matches on the table. (Or use a battery-operated candle.)

- Provide paper and pencils or pens.

- Post a copy of the mission of the church.

- Post a copy of the description of a disciple that you worked on in Step 5.

- Have a large supply of 3 x 5 sticky notes for Discovery Activity 2.

- If possible, arrange to leave the sticky papers from Activity 2 on the wall for team members and others in the congregation to see during upcoming weeks.

- Make copies of Bible Study for Step 6 and Bible Study for Step 7, which is to be handed out at the end of this session and worked on at home. Also, make copies of Individual Preparation to send home.

- You may want to engage other members of the congregation to work with the team on Discovery Activity 2. We suggest working the activities first as a team; then have the members lead the activities with other groups.

> ### More Than One
>
> This step may require more than one meeting. Plan to invest the extra time.
>
> Discovery Activity 2 will take a large amount of time. If you need to divide this step into two sessions, after Activity 2 may be the best place to do so. Plan an opening and closing worship for each session.

 YOUR CHURCH: If you are a small church, you may want to involve the whole congregation in this step.

Worship

- Light the candle and remind the group of its meaning and that anyone may blow it out and relight it if at some time during your time together you do not act or speak as you would if Christ were physically here with you.

- State together the mission of the church:

    To make disciples of Jesus Christ for the transformation of the world.

- Read the centering prayer together, or have someone read it while the group meditates.

- Ask where they have seen God at work in their lives or in the life of the church since last you met.

- Ask someone to read Acts 14:26-28. Tell the team members that this Scripture is about Paul and Barnabas reporting to the church at Antioch as to just how God had been at work in their ministry.

- Pray a prayer similar to this: Our God, we ask that you be with us today as we look at the various ministries and activities that our church carries out. Help us to see how they fit into the mission of the church, to make disciples of Jesus Christ. Amen.

Discovery Activity 1

Ask people to share any metaphors they wrote about or drew as they prepared for this session. Receive all the ideas; make a list. At this point, you do not need to agree on a specific metaphor. The team will have strong agreement and enthusiasm when a metaphor for your congregation is discovered. Remind people that God works among them and in the congregation to reveal the path of discipleship for you context.

Bible Study

Distribute the Bible Study for Step 6 and work through it together. Record the ideas that are generated in discussion so that you can refer to them throughout the rest of the session.

Discovery Activity 2

- Distribute 3 x 5 sticky notes and ask people to write one activity your church does on each note from the list they compiled as they prepared for this step.

Give them some examples as starters: worship; Sunday school; organizations for women, men, youth; a rummage sale, special collections, an annual fish fry, church camp, Vacation Bible School, a volunteer choir, administrative meetings. Don't leave anything out.

- Put all the sticky notes on a wall or large paper. Ask individuals to bring forward their notes and read them out to the group. Put duplicate notes on top of each other. As the notes are read, add activities others remember and call out.

Keep going and list everything. Some people might remember things you used to do. List them all. Don't cut this phase short. Make sure everyone has time to think about all the things. If someone has not spoken up, call on him or her gently: "Don, what are you thinking?"

Do NOT evaluate anyone's comments. Just add them to the list. Keep the brainstorming freewheeling at this stage. When the contributions begin to slow down, thank everyone for their memories, and **take a break**.

• Now the group will evaluate each item on the list. Remember, you are neither evaluating what people have said nor anyone's memories. You are evaluating the long list of things your congregation does.

• Remind everyone of the mission of the church and your description of a disciple.

• Evaluate whether the things your congregation does help make disciples. A simple "yes" or "no" will not work, because many of those activities have several outcomes. Consider the PRIMARY focus of each.

• Mark each thing you have listed with one of these symbols:

  ○ **AMD**—Actively Makes Disciples: Things that we as a church do to specifically make disciples, such as a weekly Bible study in a prison or a Bible 101 class for people first coming into the church or a VBS in a deprived neighborhood. Actively making disciples is the primary aim of this event.

  ○ **MDS**—Makes Disciples Secondarily: An activity not designed for us as a congregation to make disciples directly, but by our doing this ministry some persons may become disciples or grow in faith. An example would be contributing money as a congregation to the local agency that helps the homeless.

  ○ **FOB**—For Our Benefit: These are the things the church does for the benefit of our own members, often for fun and fellowship. The regular fifth Sunday covered dish dinner might be an example of this. And, no, there's nothing wrong with a congregation doing FOB events, they build community and unity.

  ○ **TPB**—To Pay Bills: These are the things we as a congregation do to pay our bills, to make building improvements or add to the building fund or perhaps to share some income with missionaries or helping agencies. The annual church fair, the rummage sale, and the car wash might be examples of this. Here's a hint: TPB's are those activities in and through which we as a congregation ask other people outside the congregation to help support the church. And paying our bills is important because it enables us to do the other things.

Here's a warning: Some things are not going to fall neatly into one or another category.

What about Sunday morning worship, for example? We do that for the benefit of the church members and we hope that church members will grow in discipleship as a result of participating in worship. But whether or not our services of worship are primarily for our own benefit or are genuinely aimed at making disciples depends on how open—*how honestly open*—our services of worship are to the newcomer; the stranger; the person who looks, dresses, acts, and is different from the rest of us; and to those who speak a different language or come from another culture or country. Struggle with this assessment; it's not easy.

So what do you do with these things we do that don't fit neatly into just one category? Don't worry. Put a marking on them for every category in which they seem to fit. But don't stretch too far! Yes, a person might start coming to our church because of our lawn fair in the spring, but the purpose of our lawn fair is probably not to make disciples; it is to raise money for the church, right?

However, one church used their large garage sale to offer tours of the church building. Clowns milled among the crowd, inviting people to take the tour. On this tour they gave the history and ministries of the church, as well as some information about their worship services. Another church sold Christmas trees and gave a "Trimming the Tree" devotional as well as information about the church to each person who bought a tree.

When you have completed this activity, save the notes for Discovery Activity 3.

Discovery Activity 3

• Repeat together the mission of the church: **To make disciples of Jesus Christ for the transformation of the world**. Then remind everyone of the definition of disciple that you developed earlier. Repeat it.

• Now the fun begins! You will begin to build the framework for your congregation's intentional disciple formation process. Remind the group of your conversation in Step 5 about the stages of growth in faith: John Wesley talks about people who experience God's grace in different ways. Review the stages you discussed. In the preparation for this step, you read about people who are outside the influence of the church, cautious, curious, committed, professing, and inviting others to the faith. What will you call the stages of faith for your congregation?

• The framework for planning your discipleship system will be a two-dimensional grid. Across the top of a large piece of paper, write the stages of faith you will use for your congregation. Choose stages of faith you want to address in your discipleship system. Consider language that will be inviting and appropriate for your congregation. Here are some possibilities:

	Seekers	**Believers**		**Inviters**	
		OR			
Cautious	**Curious**	**Committed**		**Professing**	**Inviting**
		OR			
Unchurched	**Curious**	**New Believer**	**Seasoned**	**New Paradigm**	**Fully Committed***

* From *Deepening Your Effectiveness: Restructuring the Local Church for Life Transformation,* by Dan Glover and Claudia Lavy (Discipleship Resources, 2006).

• The second dimension of your grid will be the elements of discipleship you think are important for your congregation. Look again at your description of a disciple. What is needed to help people grow toward your description? Down the left side of the paper on which you are creating a grid, list three to five values or practices you determine will be the way to grow in discipleship. One possibility comes from the vows to support our congregations with prayers, presence, gifts, service, and witness. You might choose to list the categories in the book *Five Practices of Fruitful Congregations*, by Robert Schnase (Abingdon Press, 2007): Hospitality, Worship, Faith Development, Mission and Service, and Generosity. Remind the group that John Wesley's classes at every level involved prayer, accountability, and teaching.

Here are some examples of grids:

	Seekers	Believers	Inviters
Prayer			
Service			
Learning			
Worship			
Giving			

Or your grid might look like this:

	Cautious	Curious	Committed	Professing	Inviting
Know God					
Love God					
Serve God					

Using Glover and Lavy's stages listed above and Schnase's faith practices along the side, a grid might look like this:

	Unchurched	Curious	New Believer	Seasoned	New Paradigm	Fully Committed
Hospitality						
Worship						
Faith Development						
Mission & Service						
Generosity						

When you have created a grid, remind the team that this is a work in progress. You are making *great* progress, but you can still adjust categories. God will continue to work with you and the people in your community and new ideas may emerge.

- Stand back to look at the grid you have created. Now look again at the sticky notes with all the things you are already doing in your congregation. Invite the team to put the sticky notes in the grid where they think it is most appropriate.

Here is one more grid to illustrate the way existing ministries might engage people at various stages of faith:

	Cautious	Curious	Committed	Professing	Inviting
Know God					
Love God				Disciple I	
Serve God			Habitat for Humanity Build		

As you can see, Disciple I is a possibility for a "professing" Christian in the "Love God" category, while working on a Habitat house is a way of serving for a "Committed" Christian. Continue to place ministries throughout your tool. Note that not every ministry the team identified will fit into a category.

Once you have completed this task, you will have a good overview of what the church currently does to form disciples. Take time to celebrate those ministries you already have in place.

Note to facilitator: As the team is working, there may be spontaneous comments about the way your present ministries fit in the grid. Be sure to capture those comments. In the next step you will revisit the grid to evaluate your present ministries and plan for the future.

Save the work you have done to complete the rest of the steps.

Closing

State together the mission of the church:

To make disciples of Jesus Christ for the transformation of the world.

Read again, or have read, Matthew 28:16-20.

Ask: How will the work we've done during this step "make disciples for Jesus Christ for the transformation of the world"?

Remind the team of their role of sharing what they are doing with the congregation. Tell them that as you move forward in planning and implementing your plans, they might meet resistance from members of the congregation as you reshape ministry and introduce new ministry. Prepare the team to respond to questions from the perspective of the mission. Encourage them to listen deeply, respond in a compassionate way, pointing to the mission, and show, if possible, how the changes build on the foundation of the past.

Close in prayer, in whatever way seems appropriate, and read this benediction together:

> *May the Lord make your love increase and overflow for each other*
> *and for everyone else, just as ours does for you.*
> (1 Thessalonians 3:12, NIV)

Remind the team members to be in prayer about the mission and to continue to reflect on what you've covered in this step, thinking about how each activity of the church does or does not fulfill the mission. Remind them to ask their prayer partners for special prayers as you continue.

Hand out Individual Preparation for Step 7 **and Bible Study 7** and ask them to study both before the next session. Tell them that the Bible study will take more time than some Bible studies and to plan accordingly.

LEADER/FACILITATOR: Create a list from the sticky notes; email it to team members in the next day or two. Suggest that they continue to think about how each activity of the church does or does not fulfill the mission. Ask them to think about the areas your church needs to focus on in order to make disciples of Jesus Christ.

TEAM: Review the list between now and the next session. Share your findings with members of the congregation.

PASTOR: Continue to participate in these important sessions. Continue to cast the vision. Continue to listen for and solicit congregational input.

INVITING THE CONGREGATION: Write a brief article to communicate to the congregation what you did in this step. Even if you involved additional members of the congregation, some may not have been able to participate. Also, help the church membership understand that forming and implementing a disciple formation process will take time and that they need not expect to be finished in a year. Disciple making takes a lifetime.

CHECK YOUR BEARINGS: How did naming the current reality of your church go? A reality check can show a congregation that they do some, little, or no ministry toward the formation of disciples. What life-giving ministries does your church already have in place? Did you find a way to celebrate that fact? Did the group discover present disciple formation efforts that need to be fine-tuned? Sometimes, facing the current reality can be demoralizing. If that was the case, how can you help the group move forward?

Bible Study for Step 6

When the crowd heard this [Peter's address to the Pentecost crowd in Jerusalem], they were deeply troubled. They said to Peter and the other apostles, "Brothers, what should we do?"

Peter replied, "Change your hearts and lives. Each of you must be baptized in the name of Jesus Christ for the forgiveness of your sins. Then you will receive the gift of the Holy Spirit. This promise is for you, your children, and for all who are far away—as many as the Lord our God invites." With many other words he testified to them and encouraged them, saying, "Be saved from this perverse generation." Those who accepted Peter's message were baptized. God brought about three thousand people into the community on that day.

The believers devoted themselves to the apostles' teaching, to the community, to their shared meals, and to their prayers. A sense of awe came over everyone. God performed many wonders and signs through the apostles. All the believers were united and shared everything. They would sell pieces of property and possessions and distribute the proceeds to everyone who needed them. Every day, they met together in the temple and ate in their homes. They shared food with gladness and simplicity. They praised God and demonstrated God's goodness to everyone. The Lord added daily to the community those who were being saved.

(Acts 2:37-47, CEB)

• Where do you see your congregation's journey with Jesus reflected in this passage?

• Which of the practices described in the last paragraph are you engaged in? Which have you observed others in the congregation engaged in?

• Which practices in those verses do you find the most difficult? Which are easy for you?

• This passage reflects early church life. Where do you see this life lived in your congregation?

Individual Preparation

Read this ahead of time, and bring it with you to our Step 7 meeting.

Centering Prayer

Wise and truthful God, you lay the path ahead for us, that we might know your will. Guide and direct us as we seek to discover the path. We want to see who you envision us to be. Help us to stop, listen, and hear your voice. Be the lamp for our feet and the light leading us to see you at the end of the path. We pray in Jesus' name, who is the Way, the Truth, and the Life. Amen.

Scripture

> *I am about to do a new thing; now it springs forth, do you not perceive it?*
> *I will make a way in the wilderness and rivers in the desert.*
>
> (Isaiah 43:19, NRSV)

Reflections

That last session was kind of fun, wasn't it? We discovered that we do a lot more than we realized. Our calendar is filled with many "things." But we may now realize that some of the things we do are not very effective in fulfilling the mission of the church.

What was that mission of the church again?

> **The mission of the church—our church—is to make disciples of Jesus Christ for the transformation of the world.**

We've also said that the church carries out that mission by doing "things," that is, by engaging in ministries.

We've identified all the things our congregation does, or at least most of them, and we've grouped those according to categories we set up. You've probably come to realize that some kinds of persons are not included in our congregation's ministries.

Now where do we go from here? In this preparation, we'll be thinking about where we want to go into the future. Thinking about what our church will look like in the future might be a good place to start.

You have started to think about a metaphor for an intentional discipleship system. Now we want to think about what we as a church will be like if we were filled with disciples. As you prepare for our next step, ask yourself:

- If our congregation were serious, really serious, about making disciples of Jesus Christ, what would our congregation be doing in five years?

- What would our congregation be doing that it is doing now?

- What would our congregation be doing that it is not doing now and perhaps has never done?

• What are we doing now that we probably wouldn't be doing in five years because these things do not contribute to making disciples of Jesus Christ?

• How would our community be different in five years because our church would be filled with real disciples?

Get the idea?

We want to think about where we want to be and what we want to be doing in the future. This is a description of where we want to be and what we want to be doing *as seen through a particular "lens."* And the "lens" is the mission of the church: **Making disciples of Jesus Christ for the transformation of the world.**

Some writers have said the mission is like the frame of the window through which we look at the future. You use the metaphor that communicates most effectively with you. In other words, describe what we want the future to look like *in terms of our mission— in terms of making disciples of Jesus Christ for the transformation of the world.*

We may hope that the church gets new choir robes in the next five years. But if we look at the future through the lens of the mission statement—making disciples of Jesus Christ for the transformation of the world—does the expenditure of energy and resources on choir robes "pay off" in terms of fulfilling the mission of the congregation as much as, say, an active bus ministry in the public housing project across town?

In five years we might hope for a new fellowship hall where we can hold covered dish dinners for the congregation and have a place for our children and youth to play basketball. But if that new building is seen through the "lens" of the mission statement, we might modify that vision to include setting up a ministry of meals and overnight accommodations for the homeless in your community and holding "open gymnasium" three nights a week so that *all* the neighborhood children can have a place to play and "hang out" that is safe, supervised, and Christian – a place where the love of Christ can be put into action.

Programs, Not!

By the way, a congregation is not involved in "programs." Programs are what we watch on television and activities undertaken by social clubs and organizations. The church is involved in *ministries*. A working definition of *ministries* might be: *Those activities by and through which persons both within and outside the congregation grow in Christian faith and discipleship.* Does that definition of ministries cause a bit of an "ouch"?

Every congregation comes to realize sooner or later that some of the things on which it spends its time, resources, and energy do not contribute to growth in Christian faith and discipleship. The classic question then is: "Why are we doing these things?" Better have some good answers! We'll be talking about the church's ministries throughout the rest of our time together; we'll leave the word "programs" to others.

Does new carpeting in the ladies' parlor contribute to making disciples as much as volunteering at the local shelter for women and children? Does the men's annual fishing trip contribute as much to making disciples as challenging those men to take some fatherless kids fishing on a regular basis, demonstrating the love of Christ through their lives and service?

These examples are ways of looking at what we might be doing. Are you beginning to get the idea here?

When we dream about the future and start to paint a picture of what we want it to look like, we paint that picture *in terms of the mission of the church*, in terms of making disciples of Jesus Christ for the transformation of the world.

Before our next meeting, think about what our church might be doing in the next five years to transform our church, our community, and the world.

May the Lord make your love increase and overflow for each other
and for everyone else, just as ours does for you.
(1 Thessalonians 3:12, NIV)

Bible Study for Step 7

(To be used at home before the next session.)

Jesus said to his disciples:

I am the true vine, and my Father is the gardener. He cuts away every branch of mine that doesn't produce fruit. But he trims clean every branch that does produce fruit, so that it will produce even more fruit. You are already clean because of what I have said to you.

Stay joined to me, and I will stay joined to you. Just as a branch cannot produce fruit unless it stays joined to the vine, you cannot produce fruit unless you stay joined to me. I am the vine, and you are the branches. If you stay joined to me, and I stay joined to you, then you will produce lots of fruit. But you cannot do anything without me. If you don't stay joined to me, you will be thrown away. You will be like dry branches that are gathered up and burned in a fire.

Stay joined to me and let my teachings become part of you. Then you can pray for whatever you want, and your prayer will be answered. When you become fruitful disciples of mine, my Father will be honored. I have loved you, just as my Father has loved me. So remain faithful to my love for you. If you obey me, I will keep loving you, just as my Father keeps loving me, because I have obeyed him.

I have told you this to make you as completely happy as I am. Now I tell you to love each other, as I have loved you. The greatest way to show love for friends is to die for them. And you are my friends, if you obey me. Servants don't know what their master is doing, and so I don't speak to you as my servants. I speak to you as my friends, and I have told you everything that my Father has told me.

You did not choose me. I chose you and sent you out to produce fruit, the kind of fruit that will last. Then my Father will give you whatever you ask for in my name. So I command you to love each other.

(John 15:1-17, CEV)

Make yourself comfortable in a place where you will not be disturbed. Take some deep, cleansing breaths, and invite God to grant wisdom and insight to you as you reflect on the Bible passage.

Slowly read the passage aloud in a quiet voice. (You might read it in different translations.) Let the words you read quench your spirit. As you hear your own voice reading the Scripture, listen for God. Listen for a word or phrase that "grabs" you.

Meditate on the Scripture. Think deeply about it. You may find it useful to write down some of your ideas:

• What was it about that particular spot in the passage that "grabbed" you?

• Try to put yourself into the story as one of the characters, or as the speaker.

• What are you experiencing as you immerse yourself in the passage?

• What is this passage about?

• How do you personally relate to what you're reading?

• What is God trying to say to you or invite you to in this passage?

Engage in prayer in whatever is your typical style. Share with God your thoughts, feelings, what you've discovered in the times of reading and meditation, whatever comes to mind and heart. Remember to listen too. You may wish to write your prayers. Spend whatever amount of time seems appropriate for you. Then move on.

Contemplate silently. Be still in God, giving your mind over to God, while your spirit worships God.

Begin with two or three deep, cleansing breaths. Then start to repeat a word prayer. This might be a phrase from Scripture, or maybe the words that "grabbed" you as you heard the Scripture read. It might be a one-sentence prayer or a favorite name for God. Use this "word prayer" to redirect your contemplation whenever other thoughts come into your mind. End this time with care.

Slowly come back to your conscious state, perhaps pray The Lord's Prayer, whatever seems appropriate.

Step 7

TURNING THE COURSE

Where Do We Want to Go?

After learning about discipleship, working with disciple-making systems, and reviewing your own status, you are ready to pause to focus, discern, and envision what God is calling your church to do. This discernment will happen in the context of reflection on Scripture, your mission, your vision, your core values, and on the answers to a series of questions. You may decide to include a larger group in some of this step.

Wise and truthful God,
You lay the path ahead for us, that we might know your will. Guide and direct us
as we seek to discover the path. We want to see who you envision us to be.
Help us to stop, listen, and hear your voice. Be the lamp for our feet and
the light leading us to see you at the end of the path.
We pray in the name of Jesus, who is the Way, the Truth, and the Life.
Amen.

Step 7 at a Glance

Goals

- Review your current ministry through the framework of intentional discipleship.

- Determine where God is calling your church to go in working with this disciple formation process.

- Capture some of the common phrases, images, and themes of your discussion to use in communicating the plan to the congregation.

- Consider the use of a metaphor in developing your disciple formation process.

Possible Format

- Worship

- Discovery Activity 1

- Bible Study

- Discovery Activity 2

- Closing

Preparation

- Place a candle and matches on the table. (Or use a battery-operated candle.)

- Make copies of Individual Preparation for the next session.

- Make a few additional copies of the Bible study for this step. Most members will have their own copies from their work at home, however.

- Be prepared to introduce and lead discernment as outlined in this step.

 YOUR CHURCH: If you are a small membership church, you may want to involve the whole congregation in this step.

Worship

- Light the candle and remind the group of its meaning and that anyone may blow it out and relight it if at some time during your time together you do not act or speak as you would if Christ were physically here with you.

- State together the mission of the church:

To make disciples of Jesus Christ for the transformation of the world.

- Read the centering prayer together, or have someone read it while the group meditates.

- Ask where they have seen God at work in their lives or in the life of the church since last you met.

- Pray a prayer similar to this: O God, our Creator, we ask that you give us a vision of the new thing that you have for us as your church. We are serious about making disciples for Jesus Christ for the transformation of the world, but we know that we must have a new vision. Amen.

Discovery Activity 1

- Ask the team to each create a newspaper headline about your church that might be printed today. You might suggest that a reporter is coming to church to find out what is happening. This team has listed the ministries of the church, created a description of a disciple, and embraced the mission of the church. Team members are the experts for the reporter! What will they say? Give them opportunity to share their headlines.

- Collect the headlines to use later in Step 9.

- During the sharing, summarize the journey of the team so far. As you (the facilitator), listen to the comments, review again the mission of the church, the description you have developed of a disciple, our Wesleyan heritage, and other discipleship systems in contemporary congregations. Remind the team that they will develop their own approach and not adopt someone else's.

- Turn attention to the grid developed in the last session. Begin an assessment of your current ministries by observing the grid. Here are some questions to guide the discussion:

  ❍ Notice which categories on the grid contain the most items and which the least.

  ❍ Where is the primary focus of current ministry? On making disciples? Raising money? For benefit of the congregation?

  ❍ What age levels are getting the most attention with current ministry?

  ❍ Are there people we aren't reaching? What kinds of persons? Consider age levels, marital status, socio-economic level, educational background, church (or lack of church) background, persons new to the faith, those ready to go deeper, and so on.

❍ Does our current ministry allow for multiple entry points?

❍ Do our ministries move people further along in practicing their faith?

❍ What ministries do we engage in that take both time and resources, but do not contribute to the formation of disciples? What resources do we have that we are not using to make disciples?

Remember that you are not evaluating persons or what persons have said; you're not going to evaluate people's memories or understandings. You're going to evaluate that long list of things that your congregation does or has done in the past.

• Ask someone to take notes so that you can remember what you've said as you plan for the future.

Bible Study

The team members will have worked through this Bible study individually at home. Ask for volunteers to say how this study experience was for them and to share any insights they had. Emphasize the thought that all that we do, all of the fruits of our work, must be envisioned and done through Jesus Christ. Explore the idea that fruitfulness becomes a measure of effectiveness for specific ministries.

Discovery Activity 2

• Begin to imagine a future when your congregation has an intentional discipleship system in place. Dream! Imagine! Reach out! But don't, don't let anyone critique or comment on ideas as they are suggested. This phase is not the time for naysayers or critics. This is not the time for those whose favorite line is, "It'll never work here." This is not the time for those who want to argue, "It's not in the budget," or "How could we afford to do that?"

• Ask some of the following questions. You do not need to use all of them; determine which questions fit where your team is. Capture the answers on newsprint. Use the discernment process. Discernment is not about taking a vote, thereby creating winners and losers. It's about honest speaking and honest listening. It's about hearing God's voice through others. It's about agreeing with God's direction and then moving forward together. This time is sacred. Stay attentive to the spirit of God as it comes through the members of your team in their reflection.

❍ What are the needs in our community? What does our church need to be for "such a time as this" (Esther 4:12-14)? For whom or what do we need to speak up and take action?

❍ What could be ahead for our church as we take seriously the call to make and grow disciples?

❍ What would our church look like if people were really living as disciples, as we've defined disciple?

❍ What is God calling our church to do?

❍ What does God want our Christian community to look like in five, ten, or twenty years?

❍ What, in our church's history, speaks to our future?

❍ How would our community be different if our church folks were living out our definition of disciple in their daily lives?

❍ If our congregation were serious, really serious, about making disciples of Jesus Christ, what would our congregation be doing in five years?

❍ What would our congregation be doing that it is doing now?

❍ What would our congregation be doing that it is not doing now and perhaps has never done?

❍ What are we doing now that we probably wouldn't be doing in five years because these things do not contribute to making disciples of Jesus Christ?

• Now, capture some of the images you've worked with. You might start your visioning something like this, "In five years, our congregation will . . ." Remind people that the mission statement is like the frame of pictures and the vision is the picture in that frame. The mission is "to make disciples of Jesus Christ for the transformation of the world." Encourage people to describe the picture they imagine for your congregation. Encourage them to describe the details of the picture they see—how will the disciples be formed? What ministries will be happening?

A Five-Year Plan

Why five years? If you set six months or a year for your goal, you and your congregation may grow frustrated with your inability to bring about all that you'd like to accomplish in such a short term. But if you look really long-range—say ten to fifteen years—then everyone can sit back and say, "Don't worry; we have plenty of time to get started on those ministries." And often the hidden agenda is, "We'll wait until we get some new and active members to get started on those ministry ideas." You know what happens. The new active members do not come. Why? Because you as a congregation are not doing anything to make disciples of Jesus Christ. You're right; it is a vicious cycle.

So what's a good time frame? Most writers in this area suggest three to five years, with five years being most often cited. Five years is manageable, but not so much time that you can afford to put things off. Five years is a reasonable amount of time to expect that the core members of your congregation will still be a part of your church. Five years is enough time for some significant things, really significant things, to take place in your congregation. Here's an example of a plan:

In five years, our congregation will minister directly to post high school young adults through:

• *Church leaders spending time in places young adults frequent.*

• *A bi-monthly "Christian fun and fellowship" night to which our post high school young adults can and will invite their friends.*

• *A weekly Bible study built around the needs, interests, concerns, and opportunities of young adults. This will be at a time and place convenient for young adults.*

• *A monthly outreach project designed by and for post high school young adults.*

One way to get your group started on this task is to go back to that list of "target audiences," folks you identified as not being served (or served very well) by your church. List them first, then list under each "target audience" a particular and specific ministry that you want to be doing in five years to reach that audience. Go through this process with the several kinds of audiences you as a group identified.

Another way to do this is to choose an existing ministry and think about ways it can actively make disciples.

 YOUR CHURCH: If you are a small membership church, do not feel you must put an activity in every box or category. Focus on one or two places you can make disciples more effectively.

• Develop the visions as fully as possible, and to conclude, ask the team members to write another headline. Imagine the reporter comes back in five years, interviewing them again about the church:

❍ What would our church look like if it were filled with disciples?

❍ How would our community be different if our members were all following Jesus as disciples?

❍ Compare the differences in these headlines and the ones written in Discovery Activity 1.

Closing

Ask: How will our decisions "make disciples for Jesus Christ for the transformation of the world"?

Read or have read Proverbs 29:18.

Ask the team members to place the headlines they wrote in Discovery Activity 2 around the candle.

Say something like: "Now we have some ideas about just where we want to go. In the next step, we will work on how we will get there."

Close with a prayer similar to this: Our God, we are beginning to see a new vision, and it is like water in the desert! It is a refreshing bath of freshness that flows over our parched church. Help us use this new vision to make disciples of Jesus Christ for the transformation of the world. Amen.

Read this benediction together as you close:

May the Lord make your love increase and overflow for each other
and for everyone else, just as ours does for you.

(1 Thessalonians 3:12, NIV)

Ask the team members to be in prayer about the mission and to ask their prayer partners for special prayers as you continue. Hand out Individual Preparation for Step 8, and remind them to study it before the next session.

LEADER/FACILITATOR: Help the others understand the practice of discernment. It is not voting, but honest and prayerful discussion. It usually leads to consensus, with individuals giving in some way so that the result is something everyone can agree to. Discernment can take time, so be patient.

TEAM: Listen actively to one another, ask hard questions, and be willing to push the edges of conventional "church thinking." Be prayerfully discerning what is truly a vision from God.

PASTOR: Take the lead on teaching and equipping the team for discernment and visioning. Push the team, when it's appropriate, to dig deeper in seeking God's vision, and give them permission to push boundaries. Help the team keep their focus on God. Continue to articulate the mission of the church throughout the discernment of the vision.

INVITING THE CONGREGATION: Find appropriate ways to invite the congregation to participate in the visioning and to test the vision the team puts forward. Encourage the membership to contribute in a spirit of patience and honest engagement.

CHECK YOUR BEARINGS: Is frustration welling up over the amount of time the task is taking? Don't allow the team to rush, and continue to assure team and congregation that the time to discern and seek consensus is well spent. Stay calm, and be a non-anxious presence.

Individual Preparation

Read this ahead of time, and bring it with you to our Step 8 meeting.

Centering Prayer

God of the past, present, and future, we are grateful for your presence in our midst. Our work sometimes seems difficult and tedious, but you have been right with us in the midst of it all. We thank you for your abiding love that keeps us focused on you and your vision for us. Help us to keep our work faithful to you. May it embrace your mission and vision, and may it bring about the making of lifelong disciples of Jesus Christ, in whose name we pray. Amen.

Scripture

> *Show me your paths and teach me to follow; guide me by your truth*
> *and instruct me. You keep me safe, and I always trust you.*
>
> (Psalm 25:4-5, CEV)

Reflection

We are doing just fine! The ideas are flowing, the ministries are being described, enthusiasm is swelling. Wonderful! That's just what is supposed to happen.

But before the members of our congregation get deeply involved in the ministries we have described as parts of our visioning, stop! Catch your breath. Pause again for prayer. And do a little evaluating.

One of the things John Wesley (one of those credited with the founding of what we know as The United Methodist Church) taught us was to be sure we are headed in the right direction before we go galloping down the road. Enthusiasm is wonderful; we need it; praise God for it. But enthusiasm needs at times to be tempered with careful review and evaluation; we need to be sure we are moving in the directions God really wants us to go, we need to be confident that the visions we have set for ourselves will truly take us where God is leading us.

And where do we want to go? (Trick question!) The answer again is: We want to **make disciples of Jesus Christ for the transformation of the world!** That is our mission. That's why we are here as a congregation. That is our reason for being. Because we are the church, we make disciples of Jesus Christ. It's what we do, and it is what we as a congregation have determined to do better and better as we as individuals and as a community continue to grow in Christian faith and discipleship ourselves.

So we have a tentative plan for making disciples. Many members of our congregation have had a hand in forming it. It's couched in the form of a vision—or more properly—a series of visions. And we are ready to dig in and make it happen. All along the way we will make adjustments as we evaluate our effectiveness and as new people join us.

Let's look at that overall plan a bit first to make sure it is consistent with what we know and mean by disciple making. What we can learn from other churches and congregations that have become successful in disciple making are some basic principles or characteristics, some "you have to give attention to these concerns to be successful" points, and some fundamental markers that will make our plan for disciple making work if followed and that will hinder our efforts if ignored. What are principles in other discipleship plans (Wesleyan and contemporary church examples) that we want to include in our intentional plan? List 3 principles here:

1.

2.

3.

A quick caveat, however: Our church and congregation cannot adopt another church's plan for ministries or for making disciples. The reasons are simple and obvious: Ours is a unique congregation in a unique community. No other church in all the world is exactly like our church, and no other community is exactly like our community. And should we be tempted to adopt another church's overall plan, remember too that that other church is unique also. No other church in the world, including ours, is quite like that church whose plan we may want to adopt and no other community is quite like the community in which that church is located.

So to put matters very bluntly: What worked for that other church will not work for our congregation! And what works for our congregation will not work for that other church! Sure, we can share ideas and insights, and we can profit from learning what others have done, we can develop and fine-tune our plan based on what we've learned from others. But our plan must be the plan for our church and our church alone!

Scholars and practitioners have studied successful disciple-making congregations from many angles, and the consensus seems to suggest certain characteristics that lead to success in making disciples. We will discuss those characteristics in our next meeting. Our task as a congregation, then, is to evaluate our plan against these characteristics to help make sure we are on the right track.

Do They Work?

Sure, "canned" or "prepackaged" programs worked in the congregations in which they were created, but they seldom transfer perfectly to another setting. They are not a "perfect cure for what ails every congregation." By all means, look at some of them, select what we can use in our setting, modify, and adapt. But focus on *our* congregation and *our* community—not on what worked somewhere else.

Before we meet, reread the description of a disciple that we wrote. Our understanding of discipleship is the focus of our disciple-making activities. We are trying to help persons become disciples by providing them with the experiences and the opportunities in which they can respond to Christ's call to grow.

Willow Creek Church built up their large membership believing that flashy programs that cost a lot of money and attracted numbers of persons would build discipleship. A large study showed this is not true. *Reveal: Where Are You?* by Greg Hawkins and Cally Parkinson (Willow Creek Associates, 2007) describes the study and findings. In fact, they "admit to making a mistake." Willow Creek now realizes that they should have been teaching people to become "self-feeders"—teaching them how to read the Bible themselves and encouraging them to do various spiritual practices on their own. For more information, go to the blog by Bill Hybels: http://www.outofur.com/archives/2007/10/willow_creek_re.html

Even very small congregations with little hope of increased attendance and membership can be (and are!) vitally involved in making disciples of Jesus Christ. Size is not the criterion; the definition of a disciple that we formulated is.

 YOUR CHURCH: A large study of United Methodist churches in 2009 showed that church vitality is not determined by size, location, ethnic context, nor theological leaning. Every church can be a vital effective congregation, making disciples who impact the world in their location. The key is to be intentional.

May the Lord make your love increase and overflow for each other
and for everyone else, just as ours does for you.

(1 Thessalonians 3:12, NIV)

Step 8

ADJUSTING THE BEARINGS

How Will We Get There?

At this point, you know what your church currently does to facilitate disciple formation, and you are trying to move from your current reality toward God's vision for your church. As you work through this step, the team will develop a plan to improve your disciple-formation process.

God of the past, present, and future,

We are grateful for your presence in our midst. Our work sometimes seems

difficult and tedious, but you have been right with us in the midst of it all.

We thank you for your abiding love that keeps us focused on you and your vision for us.

Help us to keep our work faithful to you. May it embrace your mission and vision,

and may it bring about the making of lifelong disciples of Jesus Christ,

in whose name we pray.

Amen.

Step 8 at a Glance

Goals

- To evaluate your tentative plans against the characteristics of successful disciple formation systems.

- To develop the details of an intentional disciple formation system for your congregation.

- To decide what metaphor, if any, you want to use to describe and communicate the disciple formation plan.

Possible Format

- Worship

- Discovery Activity 1

- Bible Study

- Discovery Activity 1

- Closing

Preparation

- Place a candle and matches on the table. (Or use a battery-operated candle.)

- Provide newsprint and markers and Bibles in several translations.

- Make copies of the Guidelines for a Healthy Disciple Formation Process for Discovery Activity 1, as well as Individual Preparation for the next session and the Bible study.

> **Take Your Time**
>
> Don't underestimate the importance of this step. This step could take multiple sessions.
>
> You may need one entire session on reviewing the stages of disciple formation, as this is an area where individuals often have widely varying opinions.
>
> You will most likely need a session identifying what is or should be offered in your church for each of the stages, once you've identified them. It may also take time to decide what you want to call the various stages in your disciple-formation process.
>
> Take your time with this step; it's critical that the results are solid.

 YOUR CHURCH: If you are a small membership church, you may want to involve your whole congregation in this step.

Worship

- Light the candle and remind the group of its meaning and that anyone may blow it out and relight it if at some time during your time together you do not act or speak as you would if Christ were physically here with you.

- State together the mission of the church:

    To make disciples of Jesus Christ for the transformation of the world.

- Read the centering prayer together, or have someone read it while the group meditates.

- Ask where they have seen God at work in their lives or in the life of the church since last you met.

- Read together Psalm 25:4-5.

- Pray a prayer similar to this: Our God, as the psalmist of old, we ask that you guide us this day in the direction that you want this church to go. You are indeed our hope, and we wish to follow your paths. Amen.

Discovery Activity 1

- Ask people to tell about a time when they have prayed for and felt God's leadership in a specific situation.

- Tell the group that this is exactly what you're seeking now—God's leadership in creating opportunities for making disciples of Jesus Christ for the transformation of the world.

- Ask team members to share the list of principles for disciple formation plans they created as they prepared for this step.

- Hand out Guidelines for a Healthy Disciple Formation Process (next page). Have team members read each point aloud. Ask what points reinforce their convictions and what points are new ideas.

Bible Study

Pass out the handout for Bible Study for Step 8 and work through it together. Then consider these questions:

○ Can you name a specific time when you wrestled with questions about who Jesus was or is?

○ What experience do you have of times when others in our congregation have struggled with their faith?

○ What connection do you see between Nicodemus' growing faith and what our team has done?

Guidelines for a Healthy Disciple Formation Process

- Every disciple formation process should carry out the church's mission and help lead your congregation toward attaining God's vision.

- Disciple formation systems require multiple entry points into the process since persons may enter at various points on their faith journey.

- Healthy disciple formation processes focus on the faith journey of individuals and the congregation. They focus on lifelong formation, rather than on programs that provide quick fixes. Periodic Bible studies on Jesus' work with the disciples, his encounter with Nicodemus, or the Ephesians' growth to maturity may aid in helping people understand the need for lifelong formation.

- A healthy disciple formation approach will include faith-forming ministries for all ages, including children and youth.

- Healthy disciple formation processes will incorporate some aspect of our Wesleyan heritage (kinds of grace, the means of grace, acts of piety and mercy, the General Rules, for example.)

- A healthy disciple formation plan will include spiritual practices of faith and means of grace. It will reflect the congregation's understanding of what a disciple is.

- Every level in a disciple formation plan needs to have resources identified that can help individuals move from stage to stage, increasing the flow of intentional growth.

- A healthy disciple formation plan includes periodic assessments for individuals, the church, and the plan itself.

- Disciple formation processes need an image or metaphor, which can help give voice to stages, practices, visual pictures, and help people grasp the concept of discipleship as a lifelong journey.

- Every disciple formation system must be relevant to the context in which the congregation engages in ministry.

Discovery Activity 2

The team is gaining a firm grasp of current reality and has cast a vision of a congregation full of Christian disciples who are transforming the community and world. This session will begin to develop an action plan.

Has a metaphor or image emerged for your discipleship system? If so, begin to use the imagery. Try it out and then evaluate it. Determine how well the metaphor serves the improved disciple formation process. What does it look like? How will it be used? Are there visual aids around the metaphor you want to create to help communicate its intent and message? Make sure the fit is not forced.

- Refer to the grid you developed during Step 6 and continue the discussion between current reality and the vision for growth in faith you developed in Step 7. You may want to ask questions from those two steps to cover points about discipleship, about the community and the context in which you live.

- Talk together about how you will develop the grid with new ministries, by adjusting ministries you already have and by allowing ineffective ministries to fade away. You may need to prune ministries so that the pastor, leaders, and congregation are not spread too thin. Remember some of the activities you listed earlier that are not making disciples? Many times, quantity replaces quality in our culture, but when we are forming disciples, having quality ministries is more important than the number of ministries offered.

> Remember, people will enter your church's disciple-formation process at various points.

Remind the team that some people may have just been introduced to Christ, and are hungry to learn more, but Disciple I might not be a good entry point for them. A Bible 101 course might suit them better. Others may transfer to your congregation from another United Methodist church or another denomination and have already been engaged in a systematic formation plan. How will those persons enter your disciple formation process?

- Celebrate what you are already doing!

- Now determine where there are gaps. What new ministries and opportunities do you want to add, or at least pursue adding? (Capture all this on newsprint also.) Use the questions below to stimulate your thinking and build a new reality, your plan:

  - Does the system include faith-forming ministries for all ages, including children and youth? Does it focus on lifelong formation rather than programs that offer a quick fix? Are there components for individuals as well as for the congregation as a whole?

  - How does the plan acknowledge that human beings develop their faith at different rates, levels, and stages, which may not be connected to chronological age?

  - Where does the system reflect our Wesleyan heritage of lifelong journey of faith? Does the plan include both accountability and faithful practices?

  - Does the system offer multiple entry points since people become part of the church at different mile markers on their faith journey? What are the opportunities for growth at every stage that can generate excitement, enthusiasm, and a sense of forward direction?

○ How will individuals move from stage to stage, increasing the flow of intentional growth?

○ How will individuals engage with the system? Will individuals simply join ministries that attract them? Will you develop an assessment tool for people who want to map a plan for personal growth? How will people understand what a disciple is?

○ How does the plan engage those people who are not involved so that they want to join a journey of faith? Is there a plan for people to request a class, a mentor, or a new ministry?

○ How does the plan contribute to the mission of the church and lead the congregation forward toward God's vision of a transformed world?

○ How is the plan relevant to our congregational context?

○ What is the timeline and strategy for implementing your plan? What activities simply need to be affirmed? What activities need to be refocused to more intentionally make disciples? What activities can be started quickly? What will take more time? Do you need to identify and train leaders?

○ Are there barriers to the disciple formation plan (such as prerequisites to a class)? Will there be resistance to changing ministries? What are your strategies for dealing with barriers?

Continue to work on the details of your ministry plan, but do not get bogged down in minute details. There will be parts you work on together and other parts to delegate to individuals with interest or expertise. Decide when you have enough of a framework to move to Step 9. The next step involves ways to get the whole congregation on board. This too may take several sessions, as communicating to the congregation cannot happen overnight. Allow the time to accomplish the mission and make the vision a reality.

Closing

State together the mission of the church:

To make disciples of Jesus Christ for the transformation of the world.

Read Matthew 28:16-20 again. Since it is so central to what we are doing, it cannot be read too many times!

Ask: How will our decisions "make disciples for Jesus Christ for the transformation of the world"?

Close in prayer, in whatever way seems appropriate, and read this benediction together:

May the Lord make your love increase and overflow for each other
and for everyone else, just as ours does for you.

(1 Thessalonians 3:12, NIV)

Alert the team that the next step involves ways to get the whole congregation on board. This too may take several sessions, since reaching the whole congregation will not happen overnight. You may need several weeks. Allow time, keeping in mind your goal is to accomplish the mission and make the vision a reality.

Ask the team members to be in prayer about the mission and to ask their prayer partners to continue their prayers. Hand out Individual Preparation for Step 9 and remind them to study it before the next session.

 LEADER/FACILITATOR: Be sure you have taken the time necessary to fully develop the disciple formation system, that the team can articulate it well, that it can be clearly defined through a metaphor or other communication tool, and that you have communicated the system clearly to your congregation, allowing them time and opportunity to understand, articulate, and connect with the mission and purpose of disciple formation. Recognize that the team or congregation may experience some emotional distress at this point. As you hear feedback, try to maintain a calming presence. If you are anxious, you will not be able to help dissipate the anxiety others feel. Encourage members to minister to and support one another.

 TEAM: Listen deeply to and beyond the congregation. Continue to spend considerable time in prayer and also to communicate progress to the congregation. Your intentional listening will increase the possibilities for people to own the results themselves.

 PASTOR: Be attentive to the emotional climate, using your pastoral skills as needed. Emotions may run high in the team or congregation as they deal with new ways of thinking and doing. Model being open to change and communicate through letters, newsletter articles, sermons, and teaching. You will help them overcome their resistance to change. Also, be alert for persons who need the additional help you can supply through your pastoral presence.

 INVITING THE CONGREGATION: Continue to encourage the membership to learn about the new disciple formation process and have a willingness to change. Because you have been intentional about communicating to and involving the congregation throughout your work, they may already have been making adjustments in the way they think or act in light of the mission, the description of a disciple, and the vision. Some may be resistant; others, indifferent. But many will expect something new and look forward to it, with your encouragement.

 CHECK YOUR BEARINGS: Are people resistant? Excited? Are positive—and negative—emotions high? Deal with the questioners in a loving and caring way. People may be embracing the plans, resisting changes to familiar patterns, or simply seeing understanding. Help people focus on Jesus Christ as their bedrock, realizing that even he made changes where necessary.

Bible Study for Step 8

This first passage tells of Nicodemus' first encounter with Jesus. You'll notice that Nicodemus seems to hold Jesus in a degree of high regard already. Yet Nicodemus doesn't understand who Jesus is and what his kingdom work is about.

There was a man named Nicodemus who was a Pharisee and a Jewish leader. One night he went to Jesus and said, "Sir, we know that God has sent you to teach us. You could not work these miracles, unless God were with you."

Jesus replied, "I tell you for certain that you must be born from above before you can see God's kingdom!"

Nicodemus asked, "How can a grown man ever be born a second time?"

Jesus answered, "I tell you for certain that before you can get into God's kingdom, you must be born not only by water, but by the Spirit. Humans give life to their children. Yet only God's Spirit can change you into a child of God. Don't be surprised when I say that you must be born from above. Only God's Spirit gives new life. The Spirit is like the wind that blows wherever it wants to. You can hear the wind, but you don't know where it comes from or where it is going."

"How can this be?" Nicodemus asked.

Jesus replied, "How can you be a teacher of Israel and not know these things? I tell you for certain that we know what we are talking about because we have seen it ourselves. But none of you will accept what we say. If you don't believe when I talk to you about things on earth, how can you possibly believe if I talk to you about things in heaven?

"No one has gone up to heaven except the Son of Man, who came down from there. And the Son of Man must be lifted up, just as that metal snake was lifted up by Moses in the desert. Then everyone who has faith in the Son of Man will have eternal life.

"God loved the people of this world so much that he gave his only Son, so that everyone who has faith in him will have eternal life and never really die. God did not send his Son into the world to condemn its people. He sent him to save them! No one who has faith in God's Son will be condemned. But everyone who doesn't have faith in him has already been condemned for not having faith in God's only Son.

"The light has come into the world, and people who do evil things are judged guilty because they love the dark more than the light. People who do evil hate the light and won't come to the light, because it clearly shows what they have done. But everyone who lives by the truth will come to the light, because they want others to know that God is really the one doing what they do."

(John 3:1-21, CEV)

• When, in past years, have you taken a step forward in faith?

This second passage from John demonstrates some growth in Nicodemus. He speaks up about Jesus to the Pharisees; and in so doing, he shows that his faith in Jesus is growing.

> *When the temple police returned to the chief priests and Pharisees, they were asked, "Why didn't you bring Jesus here?"*
>
> *They answered, "No one has ever spoken like that man!"*
>
> *The Pharisees said to them, "Have you also been fooled? Not one of the chief priests or the Pharisees has faith in him. And these people who don't know the Law are under God's curse anyway."*
>
> *Nicodemus was there at the time. He was a member of the council, and was the same one who had earlier come to see Jesus. He said, "Our Law doesn't let us condemn people before we hear what they have to say. We cannot judge them before we know what they have done."*
>
> *Then they said, "Nicodemus, you must be from Galilee! Read the Scriptures, and you will find that no prophet is to come from Galilee."*
>
> (John 7:45-52, CEV)

• Nicodemus spoke up about his faith in Jesus. How might you share your faith in a different way after this study?

In this third passage, near the end of John's Gospel, Nicodemus arrives after Jesus' death, bringing items to prepare the body. He and Joseph of Arimathea prepare and wrap the body and lay it in the tomb.

• As you think back over your faith journey, was there a time when you fully understood who Jesus is?

> *Joseph from Arimathea was one of Jesus' disciples. He had kept it secret though, because he was afraid of the Jewish leaders. But now he asked Pilate to let him have Jesus' body. Pilate gave him permission, and Joseph took it down from the cross.*
>
> *Nicodemus also came with about seventy-five pounds of spices made from myrrh and aloes. This was the same Nicodemus who had visited Jesus one night. The two men wrapped the body in a linen cloth, together with the spices, which was how the Jewish people buried their dead. In the place where Jesus had been nailed to a cross, there was a garden with a tomb that had never been used.*
>
> (John 19:38-42, CEV)

• What difference does a better understanding of Jesus make in how you live your life?

• Can you see the progression of the discipleship of Nicodemus throughout the Gospel of John? What does that tell you about discipleship?

Individual Preparation

Read this ahead of time, and bring it with you to our Step 9 meeting.

Centering Prayer

Ever-faithful God, you have guided us through our work together, and we have heard your voice. We have sought to be faithful in visibly laying out your design for disciple formation. As we bring this new plan for disciple formation to the congregation and seek to implement it, may you open their hearts and minds to the possibility and challenge of lifelong formation. May the power of your Holy Spirit blow through this team and this congregation, allowing us to hear and heed your call to be faithful disciples. We pray in the name of the one who said, "Come, follow me;" Jesus the Christ. Amen.

Scripture

> *Whereby the dayspring* from on high hath visited us, to give light to them that sit in darkness and in the shadow of death, to guide our feet into the way of peace.*
>
> (Luke 1:78b-79, KJV)

* The word, "dayspring" refers to Christ who brought about a new era in understanding God.

Reflections

At this point, you and the team have done a lot of hard work for the life of your congregation. At each step, you have reflected on the mission of the church, and considered the way to shape an intentional disciple formation system for the context of community life in your congregation. The team has a vision of a community that is full of Christian disciples living into God's vision of a transformed people and a transformed world. By now, we're feeling pretty good about it. Great! We must spread the enthusiasm for growing toward deeper discipleship with the broader congregation. The more each person in our group is excited about our plan, the more possibility for that visioning to become reality.

At each step, you have shared the team's work and your personal understanding with a prayer partner. There have been suggestions for engaging others in some of the steps. Hopefully, there is some "buzz" in the congregation about the work the team is doing. Here's a subtle way to measure that enthusiasm. Some call it the "parking lot test." What do folks who have been part of our group do when our group meetings have ended? Do we gather up our belongings and race home? Or do we linger, either in the building or in the church parking lot, talking, discussing ideas, sharing insights, building on plans, using our imaginations? The more folks linger to talk together after meetings such as we've been having, the more enthusiasm and excitement about the whole project there will be! One pastor had to start flashing the parking lot lights about an hour after the group meetings ended in order to break up the conversations going on in the parking lot. That's enthusiasm that spills over and builds on itself!

In this step, you will turn your attention to a plan for engaging the congregation in the development. It's important to get the whole congregation "on board"—to help everyone see the vision for a community of Christian disciples who follow God's lead into the world. The vision and enthusiasm need to spread! Let's face it: Unless the whole congregation is behind efforts to fulfill that vision, that mission **to make disciples of Jesus Christ for the transformation of the world**, is just so many nice words on so many sheets of paper.

Our vision must come alive to the congregation. This step calls us to deeper prayer, praying for God's leading as we share the vision. This is a step for changing the culture of our congregation! We want a culture in which members, regular attendees, and visitors sense a desire to join in the life with God's people who are on the move!

We want others to adopt the vision of growing closer to God over their full lifetime, never thinking that we "graduate" or "retire" in our faith life. We never want to give the impression that the team or staff is imposing new rules or formulas. Nothing can kill a vision more quickly than folks feeling that a plan has been laid upon them by someone or something else.

Whether we've had only a part of our congregation involved in the development of our plan for disciple formation so far or not, this step can only increase the enthusiasm. This step *involves the whole congregation* in getting enthusiastic about the vision and plan. Remember that people will engage your work differently, depending on their own stage of faith. Your job is not to judge anyone else's involvement, rather to point to what God is doing and can do as we grow in faith.

Be prepared that some people might want to change or "tweak" the plan. "Tweaking" simply means modifying, adjusting, perfecting, or editing the vision. Welcome new ideas, look for opportunities for conversations for exploring faith and growing as disciples. Our vision is a living, breathing vision!

OK. One of our big tasks now—all of us who have been involved so far—is getting the entire congregation excited about the vision! And we do this through *communication*. The word is simple, but the action is complex and sometimes difficult to do. Lack of communication can create significant problems. Yes, "communication" is a simple but *key* word here.

With whom is communication necessary in this case?

Breath of Life

God-inspired plans come to life when the Holy Spirit stirs our hearts with a breath of Life! Remember what happened when God breathed on a handful of dust, as reported in Genesis 2:7? That dust became alive, became a human being! And what happened when God breathed on the dry bones in Ezekiel 37? The bones began to live! In 2 Timothy 3:16, we read, "All Scripture is inspired by God." Some of the modern translations read, "All Scripture is *breathed upon* by God."

That's easy. Everybody.

Go back to that word *everybody*! What does that mean? Just what it says. *Everybody* is anyone connected in any way with our congregation. Everybody is the shut-ins and toddlers. Everybody is the youth away at college and that person who never comes to church even though that person's spouse is an active member. Everybody is the teenagers and the "golden agers." Everybody is folks who never miss a Sunday at church and the folks who show up at Easter and around Christmas. Everybody is that family that sort of "dropped out" of the congregation about a year ago but that has not since connected firmly with another congregation. Everybody is children, youth, and adults of all ages. Everybody includes members who live at far distances but who retain an interest in our congregation.

See? Even if we invited "everybody" to our meetings and the pastor preached about it on Sunday, that does not mean that *everybody* has caught the vision.

To prepare for this step of inviting others on a faith journey, let's think about the way Jesus invited people to join the vision of what he called "the kingdom of God." As you read these passages, notice words and patterns that attract your attention.

> Walking along the beach of Lake Galilee, Jesus saw two brothers: Simon (later called Peter) and Andrew. They were fishing, throwing their nets into the lake. It was their regular work. Jesus said to them, "**Come** with me. I'll make a new kind of fisherman out of you." (Matthew 4:18, Message)

> After this he went out and saw a man named Levi at his work collecting taxes. Jesus said, "**Come** along with me." And he did—walked away from everything and went with him. (Luke 5:27-28, Message).

> "Go back and tell John what you have just seen and heard: The blind see, The lame walk, Lepers are cleansed, the deaf hear, the dead are raised, the wretched of the earth have God's salvation hospitality extended to them. "Is this what you were expecting? Then count yourselves fortunate!" (Luke 7:22-23, Message)

> Nathanael asked, "Can anything good come from Nazareth?" Philip answered, "**Come** and **see**." (John 1:46, CEV)

- List other examples you can think of or find in your Bible. How did Jesus invite others into a kingdom vision?

Jesus did preach to crowds and the word spread. He also had significant one-on-one conversations. Consider how your ideas of what Jesus did might apply to the congregation. Put a check beside the forms of communication currently used in your congregation:

- A newsletter (Print? Electronic?)

- Emails

- Website

- Social media such as Facebook, Twitter

- The worship bulletin and projected announcements

- Verbal announcements during worship

- Sunday school announcements (Printed? In person? Email between class meetings?)

- Hallway and classroom bulletin boards

- Special mailings or brochures

- The local radio or television station

- The local newspaper or neighborhood magazine

- A sign in the church yard

- A highway billboard

- Informal conversations among members and conversation of members with friends in the community

What other ways does your congregation communicate? Is one way more important than another way for our particular church? Is the sermon the best way to get folks excited? Is the newsletter? Is an insert in the worship bulletin?

When the team meets for Step 9, we will build a plan for sharing the vision we have of intentional disciple making for our congregation. Remember, remember, remember: This is not the team's vision for the team's mission. **The entire congregation must see it as *our* vision for *our* mission!**

May the Lord make your love increase and overflow for each other
and for everyone else, just as ours does for you.

(1 Thessalonians 3:12, NIV)

Step 9

JOINING THE VOYAGE

Who's Going With Us?

The desired result for this step is to develop the plan to invite persons to own and engage in the congregation's disciple-formation process. Communicating to the congregation at every phase is critical. You have been encouraged to involve the congregation up to this point, so this is the next natural step. This is the opportunity to share your enthusiasm and invite others to join the journey!

Ever-faithful God,

You have guided us, and we have heard your voice.

We have sought to be faithful in visibly laying out your design for disciple formation.

As we bring this new plan for disciple formation to the congregation and

seek to implement it, may you open their hearts and minds

to the possibility and challenge of lifelong formation.

May the power of your Holy Spirit blow through this team and this congregation,

allowing us to hear and heed your call to be faithful disciples. We pray in the name of the

One who said, "Come, follow me": Jesus the Christ.

Amen.

Step 9 at a Glance

Goals

- Develop the plan for inviting others in the congregation into the disciple formation process.

- Spread the team's excitement so as to create desire among the members of the congregation to grow in their relationship with God and become disciples of Christ for the transformation of the world.

Possible Format

- Worship

- Discovery Activity 1

- Bible Study

- Discovery Activity 2

- Closing

Preparation

- Place a candle and matches on the table. (Or use a battery-operated candle.)

- Make copies of the Bible Study for Step 9 and the Individual Preparation for the next session.

- Review this checklist for launching the discipleship plan to the congregation. Are these things in place? If some of these components are missing, or you feel they are weak, you will want to pause at this point and do some additional work in those weak areas before your proceed:

  ❍ The congregation knows the mission of the church is to make disciples for the transformation of the world.

  ❍ The congregation has been involved in describing a disciple, and has a grasp of Wesleyan theology of faith development as a lifelong journey. Individuals might be starting to wonder how they can grow in faith.

  ❍ The congregation has been praying that God will open the way for deeper discipleship and more faithful following of Christ. Messages about the need for growing in faith and affirmation of ways people are already growing in faith are common in the congregation.

  ❍ The culture of the congregation has been shifting to an understanding of the importance of the connection between the various ministry activities and the mission to make disciples of Jesus Christ.

Worship

- Light the candle and remind the group of its meaning and that anyone may blow it out and relight it if at some time during your time together you do not act or speak as you would if Christ were physically here with you.

- State together the mission of the church:

   To make disciples of Jesus Christ for the transformation of the world.

- Read the centering prayer together, or have someone read it while the group meditates.

- Ask where they have seen God at work in their lives or in the life of the church since last you met.

- Read together Luke 1:78b-79 from the Individual Preparation. This translation from the King James Bible uses the term "dayspring," old English for the dawning of a new era. Invite people to imagine a new era dawning in your congregation.

- Pray a prayer similar to this: Thank you, God, for guiding us through these many steps in planning the path for our church to form disciples. We see this as a dayspring, or a new era in our church. Direct us now as we seek to bring everyone in our congregation on board. Amen.

Discovery Activity 1

- As the team considers a new era for your church, tell them that during this step you will seek God's guidance for the best way to move into it. Discerning that will require the insights of everyone on the team as how to share new ideas and introduce new plans. Remind the team that they have a special bond and a focus on the discipleship system, but others are not in the same place. Remember the factors in the sidebar about disciple formation.

- At this point, some congregations have had a special launch event. Other congregations have already engaged the congregation so that a "launch " seems anti-climatic. Some churches find it more effective not to make a big emphasis on a specific day, but to work with individuals or small groups. It is not necessary to have a specific launch event, but if you want to do so, make it exciting and celebratory! Here are some suggestions and examples:

  ○ Prepare a special worship service to introduce the discipleship system. Be sure to include the mission of the church in this service. Check the topical index of the hymnal for music suggestions under "Discipleship and Service."

> **Discipleship Formation**
> - Is not optional.
> - Is messy.
> - Is the work of the individual, the congregation, and God.
> - Will look different in each context.
> - Is for the transformation of the world.
> - Above all, is *intentional*.

○ Ask one of your musicians to either write or identify a specific hymn that will not only be used for launching this effort but will also be used at other times to identify it.

○ Publish a brochure that explains the imagery or metaphor.

○ Set up a visual display in front of the sanctuary that relates to your metaphor. For example, if you are using a tree as your theme, bring a branch with smaller branches into the sanctuary, or even a root from a dead tree.

• You may have a strong sense of the best way to communicate intentional discipleship to the congregation. Do a quick survey of the team to ask what they sense is the best way to communicate the plan.

Bible Study

Hand out copies of the Bible Study for Step 9 and work through it together. Make note of the responses during the Bible study. You will build on the foundation of your current evidence to tell people how your plan will help them grow deeper.

Discovery Activity 2

Form a plan to invite others to join the path your discipleship team has dreamed about. Make notes as you plan, collecting all the ideas. Remember that your task is to invite people to the journey like Jesus did when he said, "Come and see." Consider the questions and suggestions below to stimulate your creativity:

○ Prepare for questions people might have about the journey or about their own faith development. This is where the metaphor you have developed for a path of discipleship can help. You will be able to tell how a faith journey is like the elements of your metaphor. If you have an assessment for individuals to use to decide what to do next on their journey, tell everyone about that. Remind people that they can talk with your pastor and other church leaders about their faith and their questions.

○ Plan ways to share the "why we're doing this" over and over. Remember the "evidence" you named during the Bible study you just did. What are the ways you can share this "evidence" with the congregation? As you talk about the "evidence," tell how the plan of discipleship will provide a way for everyone to grow in faith through the years.

○ The goal of the discipleship system is that when individuals hear God's call for a closer and deeper walk with God, the congregation will have things in place to support the journey. How will you encourage people to share their experience with God and ask for what they feel God is nudging them toward? For example, if someone wants to know more about the Bible, whom will they ask?

❍ What are ways to communicate to the congregation specific ways in which the plan applies to each individual? What strategies extend both the invitation and the encouragement to each person, so that each one will be involved in deepening his or her faith.

❍ How will you communicate (verbally and nonverbally) that the intentional discipleship plan is the beginning of a new direction, not the beginning of an "event" that will come and go. It is an opportunity to reclaim our Wesleyan heritage that growing in faith is a lifelong process. The gift of God's grace is offered throughout our lives and comes to us in many ways. Make it clear that intentional disciple formation is about to become an integral part of your church from now on in all that you do, and this marks the beginning point of this new emphasis.

❍ What will you do to communicate that people can enter the disciple formation process at any point at any time? Any emphasis you implement now raises awareness of a new beginning toward intentionality in your congregation and the next step on a person's faith journey.

❍ How will you solicit testimonies from people who are growing as disciples in order to highlight why we are doing this?

❍ How will we communicate with people of all ages, including children, youth, and adults?

❍ How shall we remind people that the goal is ultimately the "transformation of the world"?

• Build a timeline now that you have lots of ideas for communicating to your congregation. Put up a clean sheet of paper. If you will have a launch-Sunday, put the date on the paper. List all the things that need to happen before the big day. What will be the follow up? If you do not have a kick-off, what needs to happen first to shift the culture of the congregation? Work on "low hanging fruit" first—pick the easy things! Whom do you need to get on board first—perhaps your prayer partners?

• Now step back to look at the plan you have developed. The next step is to write the name of the person who will be responsible for each action in your plan. Do you need to include people beyond the team who have gifts and skills for particular work?

Some have said that to communicate effectively, one must share with people seventeen different times and in seventeen different ways (the 17 x 17 rule)! That's a lot of work, *but* if the vision is not successfully communicated, the goal will not be reached.

> ### Journey
>
> To help the church as a whole see that disciple formation for all of us is a lifelong journey, consider involving the congregation in a short-term Bible study on the journey of Abraham, Moses, or one of the well-known disciples of Christ. This approach will help the congregation more fully understand that we grow continually toward the likeness of Christ— we never just "arrive."

❍ Determine how you will support one another during this step. Everyone will be busy and it will be important for you to have short meetings—even a "huddle" after worship—to share what people are saying and what questions people are asking. You may need to make adjustments in your plans. Allow enough time for everybody (there's that everybody again!) to hear about the intentional disciple formation plan and why you think it is important, but at the same time, do not drag out the communication phase. Communicate, tell the story, talk about the disciple formation plan, proclaim the excitement about the mission statement, but **know when to stop talking and start doing!**

The other side? Yes. **The other side of communication is *listening*.** The entire team needs to be listening, attuned to what's going on in the congregation:

○ Listening to conversations before and after worship.

○ Listening to conversations in Sunday school classes and small groups.

○ Listening to folks chatting in the parking lot.

○ Listening carefully, intently.

Is enthusiasm for the mission of the congregation and enthusiasm for our congregation's vision growing? Is increased excitement evident? Good! Now is the time to move onto the next phase, to take the next giant step in making disciples of Jesus Christ in and through our congregation!

Closing

Read or have read Matthew 28:16-20 again.

Ask: How will the decisions made during this step "make disciples for Jesus Christ for the transformation of the world?

Close in prayer, in whatever way seems appropriate, and read this benediction together:

> *May the Lord make your love increase and overflow for each other*
> *and for everyone else, just as ours does for you.*
>
> (1 Thessalonians 3:12, NIV)

Ask the team members to be in prayer about the mission and ask their prayer partners for special prayers. You might decide to hold on to the Individual Preparation for Step 10 until Step 9 is implemented, and then mail the handout close to the time for the next meeting.

LEADER/FACILITATOR: Be sensitive to multiple emotions the team may exhibit: excitement, success, momentum; or confusion, disappointment, rejection; or any combination of these and other emotions, depending on how the invitation is going, and how the congregation is responding. There may be parts of the disciple formation process that the team now sees will not work, and some adjustments may be necessary. Changes can create tension and frustration. Under such conditions regrouping of the team may be needed if factions arise. The team needs to experience unity. The team will need to be guided to stay focused on the purpose and not get caught up "majoring in minors." The team may also grow impatient with the amount of time it will take to move the congregation into alignment with the vision. Make refocusing as individuals and strengthening the team a priority.

 TEAM: Develop the specific plans for all the areas discussed above, and for implementing those plans. You are responsible for communicating to the entire congregation, as well as inviting and effectively receiving and nurturing individuals as they step into the process. Be active listeners and work toward positive solutions. Pat attention to the emotional climate. Everyone needs to pray for this implementation.

 PASTOR: You need to add your voice to the 17 x 17 rule of effective communication and continually cast the vision to the congregation, to small groups, to individuals, in written and spoken format, in as many ways and forms as possible and as often as possible. Perhaps a sermon series on Nehemiah and the excitement of rebuilding the wall is appropriate here. This was a new era for the Hebrew people; and Nehemiah, a common man, created excitement. (Check out this site, http://www.youtube.com/watch?v=pde5s-aF_5s, for a claymation about Nehemiah and building of the wall.) Listen to the team as well as to the congregation and readjusting as necessary. As in the other steps, your prayers for the implementation are crucial.

 INVITING THE CONGREGATION: Continue to encourage openness to the new approach to discipleship. Invite feedback, but more importantly invite the congregation to participate in the small-group sessions and other opportunities for learning about discipleship—and ultimately to enter the disciple formation process.

 CHECK YOUR BEARINGS: Has the paradigm shift begun? Is the congregation becoming engaged and fully involved? Is all the planning and development now coming to life?

Bible Study for Step 9

Go to the people of all nations and make them my disciples. Baptize them in the name of the Father, the Son, and the Holy Spirit, and teach them to do everything I have told you. I will be with you always, even until the end of the world.

(Matthew 28:19-20, CEV)

- How is your understanding of this passage similar or different to the beginning of our work on a discipleship system?

- How well do the people in our congregation understand what a disciple is?

- On a scale of one to ten (ten is the highest), can we say the congregation understands that we exist for the transformation of the world? Why or why not?

And Jesus increased in wisdom and in years, and in divine and human favor
(Luke 2:52, NRSV).

- Jesus increased in wisdom as he grew in years. What evidence do we currently have that his followers in this congregation do the same thing? How do we hope our intentional system will improve this?

- John Wesley taught that we grow in discipleship as a community and as individuals when we intentionally attend to acts of devotion, acts of justice, acts of worship, and acts of compassion. What evidence do we currently have that individuals in our congregation are intentional? What examples do we have that our congregation grows in wisdom?

Individual Preparation

Read this ahead of time, and bring it with you to our Step 10 meeting.

Centering Prayer

Merciful God, we pray that we've been faithful to you. As we review our disciple formation process, the spiritual growth of individuals and the congregation, and ongoing leader formation, keep us mindful of the vision you set before us. May the church's mission be the measuring stick by which we evaluate the disciple formation process. We pray that through this process, you have made disciples who continually grow in loving you and their neighbors. If we have made mistakes, please forgive us, and help us find ways that we can continually improve and refine this disciple-formation process to make it what you desire. In the name of Christ we pray. Amen.

Scripture

> *You are my strong shield, and I trust you completely. You have helped me,*
> *and I will celebrate and thank you in song.*
>
> (Psalm 28:7, CEV)

Reflections

Our congregation has decided to be intentional about a disciple formation process. There are definite steps for growing in faith and new ways for people to respond to God's claim on their lives. We have analyzed our context and tried to listen carefully for God's direction. We humbly proclaim, "God may be using us and the ministries we have put in place so that others may come to know God through Christ. To God be the glory!"

In preparation for the next team meeting, think about what you have learned as we worked together.

Write the mission of the church:_____

Write our description of a disciple:_____

Write down other things you have learned. Include new information you've learned, new insights about people in your congregation, new understanding of God. Over the next few days, make a list of insights you remember from this project of developing a plan for disciple formation.

Although we trust the stability of God's presence with us and around us, we know that a congregation is an ever-changing, every-becoming reality. The congregation of which we are a part today is not the same congregation of which we were a part last year or last month or last week. It will change in the future. Just like many other organisms, congregations start to die when they stand still. Congregations begin to wither when they cease to change and grow, not just numerically, but also spiritually and in terms of discipleship.

One way to maintain enthusiasm for disciple-making ministries is to recognize that our congregation is an ever-changing, ever-becoming reality. Disciple-making congregations maintain enthusiasm for making disciples *because folks can't wait to discover what new disciple-making ministries are in the works!*

Disciple-making congregations *discover new ideas for disciple-making ministries all throughout the congregation.* Ideas are not the providence of the designated leaders or the official bodies of the church. Ideas are generated throughout the congregation, and every idea is treated with enthusiasm and respect.

> Congregations provide the settings, the situations, the environments, and the opportunities in and through which persons can hear, experience, and respond to God's call and claim with a commitment to become part of the covenant community.

Disciple-making congregations *are restless congregations, in the very best sense of the word.* They are restless in that they do not rest on past achievements. Restless in that they are eager to try something new and different to make disciples. Restless in that each member of the congregation is growing in faith and discipleship, and because each member is growing in faith and discipleship, the whole congregation is always standing on tiptoe to see new ways to make disciples.

And finally, disciple-making congregations *are congregations that live in the here and now and know full well that all that they need for the future is already within the congregation today.* Disciple-making congregations are congregations who no longer make excuses. They no longer say, "If only . . ." or "We can't because . . ." Disciple-making congregations plumb the depths of the talents and skills already resident in the congregation. Disciple-making congregations expect every member and constituent to offer her or his best to the task of making disciples.

In a book titled *God's Politics,* Jim Wallis, the author, titled his Epilogue, "We Are the Ones We've Been Waiting For." That holds especially true for congregations that seriously seek to become disciple-making congregations. Those congregations long ago quit saying, "If only we could get some new folks," or "We need to get more active members in our church."

Disciple-making congregations are those congregations who know how to use every member and constituent of the congregation for the purpose of making disciples of Jesus Christ. Disciple-making congregations know that making disciples is their task, not someone else's. Disciple-making congregations focus all their energy and resources, past, present, and future, to the task of making disciples.

For that, and that alone, is the reason congregations exist.

Jesus said it: "'Go therefore and make disciples of all nations" (Matthew 28:19).

*May the Lord make your love increase and overflow for each other
and for everyone else, just as ours does for you.*

(1 Thessalonians 3:12, NIV)

111

Step 10

CONTINUING THE VOYAGE

Keeping It Going!

You've done a great job developing an intentional process for your congregation to support and increase discipleship. The initial work of your team may be finished, but the congregation is changing culture and change is on-going. This step will help you assess what you have put in place and decide how to move forward, keeping the momentum going.

Merciful God,

We pray that we've been faithful to you. As we review our plan,

the spiritual growth of individuals and the congregation, and

the ongoing formation of leaders,

keep us mindful of the vision you set before us. May the church's mission

be the measuring stick by which we evaluate our efforts.

We pray that you will be able to use work we have done to make disciples

who continually grow in loving you and their neighbors.

If we have made mistakes, please forgive us, and

help us find ways we can continually improve and refine this disciple formation process

to make it what you desire.

In the name of Christ we pray. Amen

Step 10 at a Glance

Goals

- To evaluate and celebrate the work of this team.

- To recognize that this process will continue through the years.

- To develop a plan for keeping the new disciple formation process alive, vital, healthy, and relevant for many years to come.

Possible Format

- Worship

- Discovery Activity 1

- Bible Study

- Discovery Activity 2

- Closing

Preparation

- Place a candle and matches on the table. (Or use a battery-operated candle.)

- Provide hymnals or copies of "Go, Make of All Disciples" (#571 in *The United Methodist Hymnal*) and verse 2 of "Come, Thou Fount of Every Blessing" (#400).

- Provide a variety of medium stones for Bible study.

- Read the story of the Israelites' battle (1 Samuel 7) and be prepared to tell the story (or ask someone else to do this).

- Provide newsprint and markers.

- Make copies of the Bible study and of the two handouts, Ongoing Plan for Evaluation and One Church's Plan.

Worship

- Light the candle and remind them of its meaning and that anyone may blow it out and relight it if at some time during your time together you do not act or speak as you would if Christ were physically here with you.

- State together the mission of the church:

  To make disciples of Jesus Christ for the transformation of the world.

- Sing or read together: "Go, Make of All Disciples" (#571 in *The United Methodist Hymnal*).

- Read the centering prayer together, or have someone read it while the group meditates.

- Ask where they have seen God at work in their lives or in the life of the church since last you met.

- Read together Psalm 28:7 from the Individual Preparation.

- Ask how this psalm relates to God's help in the past weeks. Encourage team members to share when they've specifically felt God's help.

- Pray a prayer similar to this: Thank you, God, for the many times you've helped us during these weeks. We're hovering between excitement and exhaustion, but give us the strength to now plan how these weeks of working with you can carry on into the future. Amen.

Discovery Activity 1

Ask team members to look at the lists they prepared for this step. Write their responses to the following questions. (Writing the notes is a way of affirming and reinforcing the contributions of each person.)

  ❍ As you think about the work we have done together, what have we learned?

  ❍ What has gone well?

  ❍ What might we have done better?

  ❍ Where have you seen God at work in our midst?

Bible Study

- Sing or read verse 2 of "Come, Thou Fount of Every Blessing" (#400 in *The United Methodist Hymnal*). Reflect on the ways God has blessed your group and your congregation during your work on intentional disciple formation. Point out the reference to an "Ebenezer."

- Distribute the Bible study and work through it together.

• Provide a variety of medium stones and ask the team members to select a stone to represent some way they have seen God help your church as you have worked. Invite each person to briefly tell about God's help they have experienced and place the stone around the worship candle as you build an Ebenezer.

Discovery Activity 2

• Hand out copies of Ongoing Plan for Evaluation and One Church's Plan. This step is important for the long-term future of your congregation as a place where intentional disciple formation continues. The development work you have done contributes to the vitality and effectiveness of your congregation into the future.

• Review the two handouts plus the notes from Discovery Activity 1. Plan your next steps.

  ❍ What recommendations and suggestions do we have for our congregational leaders (church council)?

  ❍ What suggestions will you make for ongoing monitoring of the disciple formation system?

  ❍ How will new leaders and new members to the congregation be oriented to intentional disciple formation?

• Celebrate and acknowledge the work of this team.

Closing

State together the mission of the church:

To make disciples of Jesus Christ for the transformation of the world.

Read or have read Matthew 28:16-20 again.

Ask team members to share ways their own faith has grown through this experience.

Sing a song of praise, thanking God for allowing them to have a part in the development of this disciple formation process. (Or plan some other way of giving thanks.)

Close in prayer, in whatever way seems appropriate, and read this benediction together:

May the Lord make your love increase and overflow for each other
and for everyone else, just as ours does for you.
(1 Thessalonians 3:12, NIV)

LEADER/FACILITATOR: Embrace the need for ongoing evaluation. Help train a new team or whoever will be responsible for assessment in the future.

 TEAM: Be attentive to the congregation and alert those responsible for ongoing evaluation if need be, even after their official commitment to the team has ended. Discipleship formation should be a part of each team member's DNA from here on out!

 PASTOR: Consider preaching a sermon on the Ebenezer (stone of help) mentioned in the Bible study. Continue to emphasize to the congregation their mission of making disciples for the transformation of the world. Be sure to highlight the last part of this mission ("… for the transformation of the world"), because this element focuses on reaching out beyond the church itself.

 INVITING THE CONGREGATION: Challenge the congregation to keep the mission before them in every action that they take, whether in the church building or at home or at work or simply around the community.

CHECK YOUR BEARINGS: Are the future evaluation plans in good hands? Be sure that those who will carry this forward will do so prayerfully, seeking the leadership of God.

Bible Study for Step 10

The reference to an "Ebenezer" is in 1 Samuel 7, which tells the story of the people of Israel repenting and returning to God after twenty years of worshipping foreign gods (Baal and Astarte).

The priest, Samuel, challenged the Israelites to give up other priorities (their idols) and "set your heart on the Lord! Worship him only!" (1 Samuel 7:3b, CEB)—which they did. Then Samuel asked the people to assemble at Mizpah, so that he could pray for them and they could recommit their lives to God. The people came, bringing water from their wells to pour out in a ritual of cleansing. They confessed their sin of turning away from God, fasted, and prayed.

The Philistines heard of the gathering and, as the Israelites were worshipping, their army attacked. But God was there! In the confusion, Israel prevailed; the people recognized that God had protected and guided them. They raised their Ebenezer as a reminder.

> *While Samuel was offering the entirely burned offering, the Philistines advanced to attack Israel. But the Lord thundered against the Philistines with a great blast on that very day, throwing the Philistines into such a panic that they were defeated by Israel. The Israelite soldiers came out of Mizpah and pursued the Philistines. They struck them down until they reached a place just below Beth-car. Then Samuel took a stone and set it up between Mizpah and Jeshanah. He named it Ebenezer, explaining, "The Lord helped us to this very point."*
>
> (1 Samuel 7:10-12, CEB)

• What parallels do you see between this story and the development of a disciple formation process for our congregation?

• How has God guided and protected your congregation during the time you have worked on a plan to help people grow as Christian disciples?

Ongoing Plan for Evaluation

Are we making disciples? Are we transforming our community—and the world? Our mission is always "to make disciples of Jesus Christ for the transformation of the world." The unique vision for the way the mission is accomplished in our congregation will continue to evolve as we grow in faith and our community changes in the future. The measure of a healthy disciple formation process is always "Are we making and forming disciples?"

Periodically in the future, congregational leaders must ask themselves these questions:

- Are we making disciples? Are there opportunities for people of all ages to grow in faith?

- How do we know?

- What have we learned thus far?

- What are we hearing from the people we have delegated to monitor the elements of our process?

- What can we do better? Is it time to build a team to evaluate and review our disciple formation process?

When it is time for an intentional review of your disciple formation system, here are questions to consider:

- What do written individual and congregational assessments tell us?

- What do we learn from personal testimonies shared in small groups, during worship time, and during other gatherings?

- What sermons have spoken of the process? What kind of feedback have we received?

- Are we inviting people who have yet to make a faith commitment?

- Are we celebrating our spiritual growth?

- Is the disciple formation process tied to the church-owned definition of disciple?

- Do the people in the community see the church making a difference in the community?

One Church's Plan

Here is the way one congregation set up their ongoing plan to share ideas with the whole congregation and to continue a new culture of growing as a disciple. This congregation developed the metaphor of the trail to describe their intentional disciple forming process.

As the initial work of the team was drawing to a close, they planned a **launch**, including the following:

- The chancel area of the church was transformed into a section of a trail, including a waterfall, to provide a visual for the metaphor of the trail.

- The pastor preached a six-week sermon series on the stages of faith, referring to the steps on the trail.

- All sermons were videotaped and uploaded to the website via YouTube, so they are available on an ongoing basis.

- A brochure was distributed that had been prepared, describing the steps of the trail.

- A spiritual self-assessment tool was provided for every participant in the congregation.

- A video of testimonials that had been prepared by the team was shown on two different Sundays in the worship service, sharing individual stories of people "going farther down the trail." (This video continues to be used in a variety of other ways)

- In a hundred different ways, the question was, and continues to be, asked, "What is your next step on the trail?"

To keep the momentum alive and facilitate a true culture change in the life of the congregation, the team took these steps **following the launch**:

- The original team continued to meet monthly for three months to assess and discern what was needed to keep the momentum going.

- A subcommittee was formed that called themselves the "Perpetual Motion Team" for the purpose of keeping the discipleship process in motion, creating new ideas and strategies to keep it alive.

- Members of the original team brought reports and highlights regularly to the church council members, to spark excitement and participation.

- At an all-church potluck, fully decorated with items depicting a trail theme, the congregation shared fellowship, songs, testimonies—and the pastor posed the question again "What is your next step on the trail?"

- To permeate the importance of intentional discipleship throughout the congregation, a few sessions were held with all ministry team leaders, allowing them to more fully and deeply experience some of what the original team experienced. The result from those times together was to receive commitment from all ministry team leaders that meetings would open with a deeper sense of worship and that on every agenda the question would be asked, "How did we help make disciples at this meeting/gathering?" Having this kind of commitment from ministry team leaders is crucial to keep the process alive.

- Information about and orientation to the trail is provided in many ways for the newcomers who were not part of the launch, including:

  ◯ A learning center that houses the trail and waterfall that was originally on the chancel area during the launch, with written information that explains the trail

  ◯ Detailed information about the trail on the website

  ◯ Trail brochures in newcomer packets

  ◯ Banners, signs, and other visuals present in the church

  ◯ Monthly newsletter and weekly bulletin reformatted to depict trail scenes and to highlight the meaning of the trail

- Three months after original launch, pastor preached another five-week series, describing each step on the trail, giving examples and ways to go to the next step—and help others take the next step.

- At the end of every worship service, the pastor encourages the congregation to "go forth on the trail this week, and take your next step in your journey of faith."

- T-shirts were made available for purchase that said "See You on the Trail." Special events continue to be scheduled where everyone wears their shirts.

- Announcements in the bulletin were reformatted to communicate "Opportunities on the Trail" for service, study, and spiritual growth. In many places, the suggestion is made: "Perhaps this is your next step on the trail."

- The church website received a makeover to incorporate the theme of the trail.

- An all-church picnic and hike gave the opportunity for the congregation to all journey together to the trail, complete with a "trail guide."

- The original team continues to meet quarterly to hear updates from the Perpetual Motion Team, to assess how current leadership of ministry teams is promoting intentional discipleship, to determine weak spots that need to be addressed—and to celebrate, worship together, and strengthen their own commitment to intentional discipleship. The plans are to continue to meet quarterly for the rest of this year and perhaps two times per year in the future.

CPSIA information can be obtained
at www.ICGtesting.com
Printed in the USA
LVOW04s2025220917

549758LV00006B/37/P

9 780881 776089